CW01034385

PRIDE &
PROGRESS

Dr Adam Brett & Jo Brassington

PRIDE & PROGRESS

Making Schools LGBT+ Inclusive Spaces

CORWIN

A SAGE company
2455 Teller Road
Thousand Oaks, California 91320
(0800)233-9936
www.corwin.com

SAGE Publications Ltd
1 Oliver's Yard
55 City Road
London EC1Y 1SP

SAGE Publications India Pvt Ltd
Unit No 323-333, Third Floor, F-Block
International Trade Tower Nehru Place
New Delhi 110 019

SAGE Publications Asia-Pacific Pte Ltd
3 Church Street
#10-04 Samsung Hub
Singapore 049483

Editor: Amy Thornton
Senior project editor: Chris Marke
Cover design: Wendy Scott
Typeset by: C&M Digitals (P) Ltd, Chennai, India
Printed in the UK

Library of Congress Control Number: 2023937130

British Library Cataloguing in Publication Data

ISBN 978-1-5296-1904-1
ISBN 978-1-5296-1905-8 (pbk)

CONTENTS

DEDICATION

This book is dedicated to every person who generously shared their story with us – this book is as much yours as it is ours.

ABOUT THE AUTHORS

Jo Brassington (they/them) is a former primary school teacher, now consultant, trainer, and speaker. They have used their career in education working to make educational spaces more emotionally honest and inclusive. They have a M.Sc in Teaching and Learning from the University of Oxford, and are the co-author of *Bottled: A Picture Book to Help Children Share Their Feelings.*

Adam Brett (he/him) has worked in secondary education for 15 years as a teacher, pastoral leader, senior leader, lecturer, and teacher trainer. He has a Masters in Teaching and Learning from the University of Nottingham and a Doctorate in Education from Nottingham Trent University. He can usually be found spinning around on his chair when he should be writing, or talking to his cats as if they're adults.

Together they co-founded Pride & Progress: a podcast and platform amplifying the voices of LGBT+ educators and exploring ways to reimagine our educational spaces to make them LGBT+ inclusive.

Jo tweets as @jobrassington, while Adam tweets as @DrAdamBrett. The Pride & Progress handle is @PrideProgress.

BEFORE WE BEGIN

Welcome! Thank you for making the excellent decision to read this book – we're so glad to have you here and to have you as part of the Pride & Progress community. Before we begin, we want to briefly introduce ourselves and some of the language we will be using throughout.

Hello, I'm Adam, and my pronouns are he/him.

We're so grateful to you for choosing to read our book. We hope you find it a useful and inspiring resource as you work towards creating more LGBT+ inclusive classrooms and schools. I've worked in education for 15 years as a teacher, researcher, senior leader, speaker, and trainer, and I hope my research and experience help to make this book an engaging and practical resource. I started secondary school in 1995, right in the middle of Section 28, and so as a gay person, I am acutely aware of the damaging effect a lack of inclusion and visibility can have. Inspired by my time at school, in 2021 I completed my doctorate in education, exploring the experiences of LGBT+ teachers. Completing this research was transformative and motivated me to continue this journey to support others in making their schools LGBT+ inclusive spaces. This journey really kicked into overdrive when I met the incredible Jo Brassington...

Hi, I'm Jo Brassington, and my pronouns are they/them.

I am a former primary school teacher, now a consultant, trainer, and speaker. I have a M.Sc. in Teaching and Learning, and co-authored *Bottled: A Picture Book to Help Children Share Their Feelings*. For most of my career I have been working to make educational spaces more emotionally honest and inclusive. I am non-binary, which for me means that although I was assigned male at birth, my gender identity and expression doesn't fit with being labelled a man, or the idea of masculinity more generally (all concepts we will explore in more detail later). My experience as a non-binary, queer person working in education led me to reach out and connect with other LGBT+ educators, which is how I came to meet Adam.

Together, we co-founded Pride & Progress: a podcast and platform which amplifies the voices of LGBT+ educators and explores ways to reimagine our educational spaces as more diverse, equitable, and inclusive. It is the conversations we have had through Pride & Progress (@prideprogress) which have inspired this book, but more on that later.

Throughout this book we will be using language that may not be familiar to all readers – please do not worry about this – we are all here to learn! We have a specific chapter exploring language and have tried to define terms as we use them. But before we begin, there are a few important definitions we want to share with you.

LGBTQIA+

An initialism used to represent a diverse range of romantic orientations, sexualities, and gender identities. Often shortened to LGBTQ+, LGBT+, or LGBT. We explore the letters that make up this initialism in more detail in Chapter 4.

In this book, we will most commonly use LGBT+ to refer to this community of people.

QUEER

A word historically used as a slur, or an insult, against members of the LGBT+ community. The word has since been reclaimed by the community and is now often used as an umbrella term. The word is a rejection of specific labels of romantic and sexual orientation, and/or gender identity. It is important to note that because of its historical context, this word is not welcomed by all members of the LGBT+ community.

In this book, we will use the word queer when talking with, or about, people who do identify with this term.

CISGENDER

A person whose gender identity aligns with the sex they were assigned at birth. Throughout the book we will often shorten cisgender to 'cis'.

INCLUSION

Inclusion is a broad word. In educational contexts it is used to refer to embracing all people. This may be in relation to their special educational needs, race, gender, disability, medical, or other needs. It is about giving equitable access and opportunities to all by removing barriers that may prevent this.

In this book, when we refer to inclusion or inclusive education, we will most commonly be referring specifically to the inclusion of LGBT+/queer people.

As we said, we are all here to learn, so throughout this book we would encourage you to be comfortable being uncomfortable. There may be times you experience feelings of discomfort or unease, but we want to reassure you that these are completely normal feelings. Coming outside of our comfort zone naturally causes these feelings, but it is also the place from which we grow and develop. Throughout the book, if you do experience discomfort, we encourage you to lean into this feeling and recognise that you are feeling this way as you are developing your empathy and understanding. This is a wonderful thing and something to be celebrated – if you finish this book with a better understanding of how to make your classroom LGBT+ inclusive, then we have done our job and your time has been well spent.

This is a short book designed to either be read fairly quickly from cover-to-cover, or to be dipped in and out of as you think about the specific ways in which you want to make your classroom or school more inclusive.

Writing this book has been a real labour of love and we hope you enjoy reading it as much as we enjoyed writing it.

INTRODUCTION

'Every person in a school community should be free to be themselves, to feel seen, to feel safe, to feel supported, and to feel like they belong.'

Pride & Progress

For a moment – close your eyes – and picture a school.

What did you see?

Maybe you saw classrooms, or hallways, or uniforms you hated wearing as a kid. Maybe you saw your favourite teacher, or your least favourite teacher, or perhaps you saw yourself standing at the front of class as the teacher. Maybe, like Jo, your mind immediately pictured the full-chorus cafeteria scene from *High School Musical*... or, maybe not.

It doesn't matter exactly what you pictured – the point is that everybody reading this book has a picture. Every person holds an image in their mind of what schools look like, perhaps even what they feel like. Most of us hold with that image judgements of what we believe schools should look like.

Where does this picture come from?

Each of our images are individual, and they come from our own interactions with schools. All of us have experiences in these educational spaces, which have shaped our perceptions and understanding of them. This is one of the reasons that conversations about education are often so contentious, because every person has buy-in to the discussion. Perhaps your experience is from when you navigated school yourself as a young person, more recently as a parent, or as a person who works in a school every day. Perhaps, if you're an educator like us, it feels like you never really left school.

Now, for another moment – close your eyes – and picture this time a school which is an LGBT+ inclusive space.

What do you see?

Please, take your time. Really try to imagine it. What would it look like for a school to be a diverse, equitable, and inclusive space for LGBT+ people? A safe space for all young people who occupy it, for their families, and for the adults who run it. Is the space you're imagining now similar or different to the school you imagined earlier? Is it similar or different to the schools you experienced yourself as a young person? Is it similar or different to the schools you are helping to create now as an educator or parent?

Our guess is that you probably found the second school harder to imagine, right? You were all able to picture schools because of the reference points and direct experiences you have with them. But, when it comes to imagining an LGBT+ inclusive educational space, many of you won't have these reference points, or direct experiences. This is because for most people reading this book, the system you were educated under was not LGBT+ inclusive. Whether you noticed it at the time or not, it's likely your own education did not make space for LGBT+ people, or their stories. In fact, there was legislation in place to purposefully ensure that this community of people were not spoken about in schools (but more on that in Chapter 1).

So, when we asked you to imagine an inclusive school, what we were really asking was for you to *reimagine*. To take your experiences in a non-inclusive system and reimagine them. To take an educational history of silence and shame and *reimagine* it. To take your perceptions and ideas of what a school should look like and *reimagine* them for a better, more inclusive, future.

Reimagining is not easy. There is much to consider if we are to reimagine our schools to make them LGBT+ inclusive spaces. One challenge being that reimagining anything involves equal parts learning and unlearning. We must learn new languages, new ideas, and new practices, whilst simultaneously unlearning the perceptions that our own educational experiences have built within us. Personally, we know the challenge of reimagining schools to make them LGBT+ inclusive spaces well, because we have spent years holding conversations which explore exactly that.

In the summer of 2020, as England emerged from the first of its COVID-19 lockdowns, we sat together in the window of a tapas bar in Nottingham. It was during the period of time where we were all adjusting back to conversations in real life, and the realisation that people didn't just exist from the shoulders up. In fact, this was the first time we were meeting in person, although it felt as though we knew each other quite well. For a while we had been organising or hosting online events to discuss LGBT+ inclusive education with other teachers. Through the online events we had been involved in, and through Adam's doctoral research at the time, we were beginning to hear incredible stories of educators who were quite powerfully reimagining their educational spaces to make them more inclusive. The difficulty was, as Jo put it that day over dinner, that these conversations were only ever heard by the few in attendance, and once these events were over, it felt like the conversations ended there.

We wanted a way to share these stories, to amplify these conversations, and to bring together the people who often felt like they were doing this work alone. It was over that dinner when Adam first floated the idea of a podcast. What if we recorded these conversations? What if we shared these stories? What if more people could hear about the amazing work these educators are doing to reimagine their schools? We both left that restaurant with these questions buzzing in our minds, until eventually, they became the bedrock of Pride & Progress.

When we launched the Pride & Progress podcast we did so with this statement:

> *For a while now, we have been organising events for LGBT+ educators and allies to discuss inclusive education. During these events, people shared powerful stories of pride, and of the progress being made in education. We want to share these stories, to amplify the voices of LGBT+ educators and celebrate inclusion, progress, and the power of diversity.*
>
> *We are living in a unique and pivotal moment for inclusive education. Now, for the first time ever, educators are strongly encouraged and enabled to make education, and our educational spaces, inclusive of LGBT+ lives. This requires a complete reimagining of what education could, and should, look like: an education that reflects the diverse society, allowing all people to see themselves and to feel they belong.*
>
> *Join us as we amplify the voices of these LGBT+ educators and allies, share their stories of pride and progress, and celebrate the true power of diversity in education.*

Since sharing that statement, we have curated a collection of conversations and stories from people who are all, in their own way, reimagining educational spaces to make them more LGBT+ inclusive. We have spoken to teachers, leaders, trainees, charity workers, authors, actors, and activists. Each conversation has helped us to learn, to unlearn, and to reimagine. In this book, we pull on each of those conversations, stories, and lessons to help others begin to develop the reference points and experiences needed to themselves begin reimagining schools as LGBT+ inclusive spaces. Whilst this book focuses on creating LGBT+ inclusive spaces, it is important to note that as educators our approach to diversity, equity, and inclusion should be holistic. The arguments presented in this book for greater LGBT+ equity and inclusion in schools are often arguments which benefit every person who occupies these spaces and can be used to achieve holistic inclusion.

From hours of conversation, we have drawn together ten themes that we think are the keys to reimagining educational spaces. When thinking about how to structure this book, we wanted to ensure that it gives you a clear understanding of each concept, explores what the concept looks like in reality, before helping you think about how to then apply the concept yourself. With this in mind, we have loosely adopted Rolfe et al.'s (2001) reflective model which poses three simple but brilliant questions: What? So What? Now What? These questions will be used to explore each chapter's theme under the headings of 'In Theory', 'In Practice', and 'In Action'.

The 'In Theory' section of each chapter is written by Adam, combining theory and literature with historical and current context to give you a clear understanding and vocabulary for each theme. The 'In Practice' section is written by Jo, with reference to the stories of the brilliant educators who have been part of Pride & Progress. We then close each chapter by posing questions that will allow you to think about how to apply each theme 'In Action'.

Throughout the book you will hear reference to conversations we have had on the Pride & Progress podcast. We have signposted specific episodes by following a guest's name with an S and E number, showing which season and episode they were part of. At the end of each chapter, you'll find all of the episodes which have been discussed in that section, and there is a full list of episodes in the back of the book.

This book is inspired by our experiences as educators and LGBT+ people; by the lived experiences of the people we have spoken to; and by theory and research. As with every conversation about the future of educational spaces, it is unlikely we will agree on every detail – and that is okay.

We want to thank you for picking up this book, for engaging with this conversation. Whilst you may not agree with everything we suggest in the following ten chapters, it is through these reflections and conversations that we begin to widen our understanding of what is possible in our educational spaces. So, as we enter this book, we ask you to bring your critical thinking and curiosity, but also to bring your empathy, and an open mind. We are all here with a common goal: we all want every person in our school communities to be free to be themselves, to feel seen, to feel safe, to feel supported, and to feel like they belong.

As you will hear in the following stories, we are standing on the shoulders of giants. Over the last 50 years, a small number of brave and vocal people have allowed us to make incredible strides in the fight for LGBT+ equality. We are at a pivotal moment in education, where for the first time ever, schools are being encouraged and enabled to make their curriculums and classrooms LGBT+ inclusive. We are so thrilled to have you as part of this journey and can't wait to see what we can all achieve together.

So, are you ready? Let's begin...

REFERENCE

Rolfe, G., Freshwater, D., & Jasper, M. (2001). *Critical Reflection for Nursing and the Helping Professions: A user's guide.* Palgrave.

1

SETTING THE SCENE

> *'I feel like I was cheated out of a sound start in life. I could have had those role models, I could have had books showing different family types, but there was nothing. There was absolutely nothing at that point which showed that being gay was okay.'*
>
> Helen Richardson

IN THEORY

As excited as we were to write this book, it was hard to not also feel a sense of melancholy that books about LGBT+ inclusion still need to exist. However, when you consider that in this century there were still UK laws specifically legislating that children should not be taught that it is okay to be LGBT+, it quickly becomes apparent why these texts remain vital. Most countries around the world have long and complicated LGBT+ histories; today, there are many countries that still go to extreme lengths to diminish or deny our existence. Despite its baffling logic, many governments and authorities reason that if they restrict LGBT+ education in their schools, their citizens will all magically turn out to be heterosexual and cisgender. This logic only works, of course, on the principle that being LGBT+ is a choice, proving in one sentence why this widespread approach simply doesn't work. A lot of our guests have joked that it's a wonder they turned out to be gay despite having heterosexuality so aggressively promoted to them throughout their childhood.

Encouragingly, many countries are now making positive strides with LGBT+ inclusion and have begun to ensure that LGBT+ lives are also learnt about within schools.

However, the passage of time alone does not undo the significant damage that comes from decades of state-sanctioned marginalisation and vilification. Schools need to acknowledge that LGBT+ inclusion in education has been stunted by several decades. We cannot simply pop on a rainbow lanyard and consider it job done, as we will explore in the final chapter. We must disentangle the complicated history of LGBT+ exclusion in education to ensure schools become inclusive in a way that we would expect for the 21st century.

This chapter will give a brief overview of the historical context, before positioning where we are today with LGBT+ inclusive education, highlighting the progress that has been made, and considering some of the challenges that remain. While this book is designed to be used in schools around the world, the context and examples are naturally what you would expect from two UK writers. Although UK-centric, we believe the chapter themes are universal and that the stories and advice in this book will help you to make your classrooms and schools more inclusive, whatever your context.

The 1980s were a dark time for LGBT+ people, particularly gay men. In 1987, a UK poll suggested that 64% of the population thought homosexual activity was 'always wrong' (Pearce et al. 2013). Anderson (2010) attributes this to the rise of moralistic right-wing politics, the politicisation of evangelical religion, and the AIDS crisis. Paul Baker, a guest on the podcast, perfectly captures the mood of this troubling time in his superb book *Outrageous!* (2022) which charts how the cultural temperature of the 80s led to the introduction of Section 28 in the UK. Section 28 was a pernicious and somewhat desperate piece of legislation, essentially banning LGBT+ education in UK schools, decreeing that 'local authorities shall not intentionally promote homosexuality or publish material with the intention of promoting homosexuality'. It was the first new piece of anti-LGBT+ UK legislation in over 100 years.

You can watch then-UK-Prime Minister Margaret Thatcher's chilling 1987 speech on YouTube justifying Section 28, where she proclaimed that children were 'being taught that they had the inalienable right to be gay' and that 'all of those children were being cheated of a sound start in life'. She was right about one thing, children were being cheated of a sound start in life, but it wasn't the children she was talking about. Section 28 meant that LGBT+ young people had to grow up in a culture of silence and fear, without role models or someone to turn to. LGBT+ teachers were forced into the closet for fear of 'promoting' LGBT+ lives through their mere existence, and all children were robbed of a chance to develop empathy and learn about the lives of the LGBT+ people who would be their friends, family, and colleagues in later life. Catherine Lee, a guest on the podcast, explores the impact of Section 28 in her book *Pretended: Schools and Section 28: Historical, Cultural and Personal Perspectives* (2023).

It's hard to measure the specific impact of Section 28, as sadly it seemed to reflect the national and even international mood of the time. However, what we can say is that Section 28 was a government-stamped endorsement of the homophobic and intolerant attitudes of the era which made schools a scary and isolating place for LGBT+ people, instilling a sense of fear and self-policing that continues to this day.

After 15 damaging years, Section 28 was repealed (2000 in Scotland, 2003 in the rest of the UK). The problem was, Section 28 was such a vague piece of legislation to begin with, that when it was quietly repealed, educators remained uncertain about what they could and couldn't talk about in their classrooms. As most teachers today were either educated under Section 28 or were teachers at the time, over 20 years later, we still have an education system that is dogged with uncertainty about which aspects of LGBT+ lives are acceptable to discuss. Making something 'not illegal' is not the same as empowering and educating teachers to make LGBT+ inclusion a top priority.

International research, both qualitative and quantitative, highlights that this isn't just a UK concern and that LGBT+ inclusion in education remains an issue around the world. There are numerous qualitative studies, including my own, which highlight the challenges facing LGBT+ teachers in education (Braun 2011; Brett 2021; Connell 2015; DePalma and Atkinson 2006). The quantitative studies of organisations such as the UK's Stonewall and Just Like Us, as well as America's GLAAD, highlight the difficulties that LGBT+ young people still face in schools today. Stonewall's School Report (Bradlow et al. 2017) highlights that almost half of all LGBT+ pupils still face bullying, and that more than two in five trans young people have tried to take their own life. Just Like Us (2021) identifies that LGBT+ young people are twice as likely to contemplate suicide, with black LGBT+ young people three times more likely (we explore intersectionality in Chapter 7). I identify these statistics not to shock, but to illustrate that, despite progress, schools are still often experienced as unsafe spaces for LGBT+ people.

We debated whether to include the impact that Covid has had on LGBT+ communities in this book for fear it would quickly seem dated. However, the full impact of Covid may not be known for another generation and so it's therefore worthy of discussion. Just Like Us, in their *Growing Up LGBT+: The impact of school, home and coronavirus on LGBT+ young people* report (2021), identified that 68% of LGBT+ young people said their mental health had 'got worse' since the pandemic began and that 52% of LGBT+ young people felt lonely every day during lockdown. These feelings of isolation were attributed to being denied the spaces and communities where they could safely explore their identities, as they often felt unable to do this with their families. Although this research focuses on the pandemic, the findings also help us to imagine the challenges young people face when LGBT+ inclusion remains absent in their school.

Prior to the pandemic, and in a big step forward for inclusive education, the UK government issued guidance stating that it would be mandatory for LGBT+ content to be taught within Relationships and Sex Education (RSE). The 2019 guidance stated the following:

> Schools should ensure that all of their teaching is sensitive and age appropriate in approach and content. At the point at which schools consider it appropriate to teach their pupils about LGBT, they should ensure that this content is fully integrated into their programmes of study for this area of the curriculum rather than delivered as a stand-alone unit or lesson. Schools are free to determine how they do this, and we expect all pupils to have been taught LGBT content at a timely point as part of this area of the curriculum.

Depending on your perspective, this legislation can be read as an important and much needed update to the curriculum, or perhaps more cynically, a rather vague and non-committal set of guidance. Leaving schools 'free to determine how to do this' means this work can be approached inconsistently and that the quality of LGBT+ education is largely determined by individual leadership teams and the importance they place upon it. In a brilliant move in 2021, Scotland showed they are once again a step ahead of the rest of the UK, becoming the first country in the world to embed LGBT+ education across their entire school curriculum. In 2022, the Department for Education updated the *Keeping Children Safe in Education* guidance to highlight that students who are LGBT+, or perceived to be LGBT+, are at greater risk of harm. The document also highlights that these risks may heighten further if the child doesn't have a 'trusted adult' in their life who they can be open with.

As you can see, there has been significant progress with LGBT+ inclusive education in just a few decades. While this is an incredibly short and potted history, it gives you a flavour of the challenges faced up to this point. Although the progress that has been made is cause for celebration, the job is not yet done as approaches to LGBT+ inclusion remain varied and inconsistent, even with the updated guidance. Schools are their own living and breathing ecosystems, each with their own unique contexts and challenges, where LGBT+ inclusion can range from a top priority to non-existent. There is still a lot to be done, but with the government finally acknowledging the importance of this work, there has never been a better time and opportunity for us as educators to reimagine our schools as LGBT+ inclusive spaces.

IN PRACTICE

Picture a seed planted in the middle of your school grounds.

Day after day, week after week, year after year, the seed is allowed to grow, untamed, for over a decade. The roots stretch out under the surface of the ground consuming every nutrient they come across, preventing anything else from growing. The plant stretches way above the school, towering higher and higher each year. Its dense leaves cast a dark shadow over the grounds of the school.

Granted, I have a tendency to be dramatic, but since I learnt about Section 28 this is exactly how I visualise it. The legislation was a seed of silence and shame which was planted in our educational spaces in 1988. The culture, fear, and moral panic of the time meant that this seemingly small seed was able to grow, thrive, and stretch into every corner of UK educational spaces.

Then, after 15 years when the legislation was repealed, the plant was cut down at its source – but the roots remained. The silence and shame that was allowed to grow in our educational spaces, and in the consciousness of the people who occupied them, remained very much rooted in our schools. As Adam put it: 'making something "not illegal" is not the same as empowering and educating teachers to make LGBT+ inclusion a top priority.' Repealing Section 28 did not unroot the damage caused by it.

I remember the first day I read the words Section 28 because, ironically, it was the same day I had come out to my own class for the first time. It was a Year 6 class, during my third year of teaching, and I had chosen to share my identity with them (a story I share in Chapter 9). Later that evening, as I caught up on the news, I was drawn in by one particular story. On the same date that I came out for the first time in an educational space, 16 years earlier Section 28 had been repealed in England. The irony! On the anniversary of the end of Section 28 I had become a visibly queer person in a way that teachers were prevented from doing during my own primary education.

That night I read every article I could find about Section 28. It felt like I had found the source of the silence and shame which surrounded many of my own educational experiences. I read the stories of people who were impacted by the legislation both as teachers, and as students. As I read more, 'Section 28' – which meant nothing to me hours before – began to hold so much weight.

It was through the stories and lived experiences of real people that I built empathy and came to a greater understanding. That, in a sentence, is what the 'In Practice' sections of this book are hoping to ignite. In the second section of each chapter,

I will share with you the lived experiences of our podcast guests. Through their stories, I will try to demonstrate what the theory looks like in practice. We believe it is through stories of lived experience that we best build the empathy and understanding which is required for meaningful action. In the context of this chapter, I will be sharing stories of people's interactions with Section 28 to reveal how this legislation played out in practice through people's lives.

So many of our conversations touch on the legacy of Section 28, but one of our episodes is dedicated specifically to that. Paul Baker (S2, E13) is a Professor of English Language, a researcher, and great writer. His book *Outrageous!: The story of Section 28 and Britain's battle for LGBT education* plots all that we have discussed in this chapter in greater detail. His episode is a great starting point if you want to develop your understanding of Section 28, and the impact it has had on our educational spaces.

When reading Paul's book, I was surprised to learn about the inclusion work that was already happening in schools in the 1980s before Section 28 prevented it. We hear about this in more detail from Sue Sanders (S2, E1). Sue is an inspirational educator, the Chair of the 'Schools Out UK' Charity, and the co-founder of LGBT+ History Month (which I'll discuss in more detail in Chapter 5). Teaching in London in the 1980s, Sue was out and open to staff and students, and doing equality work in her setting. She quickly became involved in the fight against Section 28. At the time, Sue and her friends explored the legal parameters of Section 28 and felt that because schools were not directly under local authority control, the legislation could not be legally applied. They sent letters to all schools making this argument.

The legal strength of Section 28 is unclear. It was never judicially tested, and no prosecutions were made. However, the fear alone was enough to silence LGBT+ lives in schools, which had a devastating impact on staff and students. Helen Richardson (S2, E2) is now a teacher, and brilliant leader, working in primary education. She was seven years old when Section 28 became law and finished her teacher training the year it was repealed. Section 28 was the backdrop to all of her early educational experiences. At 10 years old, Helen knew she was a lesbian, but she felt unable to tell anybody until she was 23. She tells us how damaging it was to not see herself reflected anywhere. The silence Section 28 created meant that Helen could only imagine one future for herself. She did everything she could to be what she was taught was 'normal', and to work towards a future where she would marry a man and have children. A future she did not want, but the only one the silence allowed her to imagine was possible.

It wasn't just the students in schools who were impacted, but the educators too. Troy Jenkinson (S1, E13) is now a headteacher, an author, and an openly gay role model.

However, at the beginning of his teaching career Troy was leading a double life: feeling unable to be honest in the classroom, or in the staff room. Troy shares a story of one day in his early career when he went into school expressing himself with a new haircut. His headteacher at the time told him that he could be sent home for the haircut. While she didn't threaten Section 28 explicitly, she alluded to it and told Troy that he must be 'very careful'. Troy felt the underlying message was that he could lose his job if he expressed himself in the workplace. Following this interaction, Troy knew he had to be mindful at all times. He would change pronouns when talking about his boyfriends and spent much of his energy concealing who he really was.

This forced concealment is sadly a common experience for many LGBT+ educators working through Section 28. Professor Catherine Lee (S2, E6) had just started her teaching career as Section 28 became UK law. Catherine describes this time as terrifying and explains how the ambiguity of the legislation only worked to heighten that fear. As fear travelled through school corridors, Catherine remembers colleagues who were 'moved on' as a result of discussing their sexuality. She found herself increasingly forced to hide herself, using her energy to safely navigate staff room conversations.

Teaching in Liverpool at the time, Catherine was out in the gay scene with her partner one Saturday night when she bumped into a student from her school. Unsure what the girl would say back at school, Catherine began to imagine losing her job. She was terrified. The following Monday she stood, overseeing the school cross country, waiting for her headteacher to summon her and end her career.

Instead, the young girl Catherine had seen in that club approached her and asked to speak about the weekend. She disclosed to Catherine that she was struggling with her own identity, and that she had been there to find other people like her. Catherine of course wanted to say, 'If you're gay that is okay, take your time, be yourself, and if you want to talk to somebody I am here.' But, with the weight of Section 28 on her shoulders, she couldn't. Instead, Catherine told that young person that she was not gay. 'It would break your family's hearts if you were, and you should never speak to me about this again.'

Catherine shut the conversation down.

She still thinks about that student to this day. In our conversation, she tells us what she would say if able to relive that moment: 'Just be yourself. It is going to be alright. Stop second guessing, stop racing ahead with your thoughts. Stop worrying. Nobody has the right to tell you who you can and can't be, and who you can and can't love.'

Can you imagine the impact this moment must have had on her as a new teacher? Or on the frightened and confused student? You can hear this story in full on the podcast or read it in more detail in Catherine's latest book: *Pretended: Schools and*

Section 28: Historical, Cultural and Personal Perspectives (2023). Her experiences of Section 28 also inspired the film *Blue Jean*.

Catherine wishes she could go back in time to change what she said, but she knows that she can't. Instead, she uses this experience to motivate her to make sure that people have better experiences now through researching LGBT+ teachers and supporting LGBT+ leaders. In our podcast she describes Section 28 as the lemons but recognises the opportunity she now has to make lemonade.

Many of our guests share this sentiment. Our podcast is full of stories of people's experiences in non-inclusive educational spaces, and how this motivates their work now. While it's important to recognise the damaging impact of our educational history, it is hopeful to see how these awful experiences are now motivating change.

These stories collectively help to reveal the weight of Section 28, and how it played out in practice through the lives of real people. While these stories are specific to the UK, our conversations on the podcast demonstrate that the history of silence and shame surrounding LGBT+ existence stretches beyond our islands. B Guerriero (S1, E5) is a primary school teacher who is non-binary, and grew up in Italy. Karan Bhumbla (S1, E6) is a secondary school science teacher who is a gay man who grew up in India. They share with us their experiences growing up in an Italian school, and a Catholic convent school in India respectively. While their stories are unique, the same culture of silence and shame is reflected in them both. The history of non-inclusive educational spaces stretches beyond the UK context.

I mentioned earlier that this silence and shame was not only rooted in our educational spaces, but in the consciousness of the people who occupied them at the time. It is because of this that we still see the shadows of silence and shame to this day. Most people who now work and lead in our schools were themselves, at least partly, educated under an education system that was not LGBT+ inclusive. Whether we are conscious of it or not, our non-inclusive educational history can still impact our views of educational spaces today.

So, how do we unroot this silence and shame from our schools? As we argued in the introduction, we believe that this unrooting requires a collective reimagining. As Adam explained earlier, we have already come some way in that reimagining, and significant progress with LGBT+ inclusive education has happened in just a few decades.

We only need to look at the experiences of those entering the profession now to see how far we have come. Scotty Cartwright (S1, E15) was at the beginning of his teaching career when we spoke with him. During his training year, he had already become involved in inclusive education work. When asked if he was gay by a student, Scotty felt safe to answer truthfully. He was honest about his identity in the interview for his first teaching position, and continues to be now in the classroom, and in the staff room. It is this trajectory which provides us with hope that things are going in the right direction.

Hope is important, and I am conscious that the first chapter of this book has not been one of hope. However, we need to explore the challenges before we present the solutions. The following two chapters will introduce you to two further challenges in our current educational context: heteronormativity and cisnormativity. We hope that in reading these first three chapters, you understand more thoroughly our call for a reimagining of educational spaces. The chapters which follow will then explore some of the solutions and themes we need to consider to continue reimagining, to continue unrooting silence and shame, and to finally create educational spaces which are truly LGBT+ inclusive. Spaces where every person is free to be themselves, feels seen, feels safe, feels supported, and feels like they belong.

IN ACTION

Having discussed the theory and research behind this theme and explored what this looks like in practice through the lived experiences of our podcast guests, we will end each chapter reflecting on what the consequences of this discussion might look like in action.

This section will pose three reflective opportunities. This reflection will look different for everybody, but we encourage you to actively engage with these questions; whether this is through individual reflection and note taking, using these questions as a basis for conversation with colleagues, or as a prompt to engage staff in CPD. We hope this engagement will allow you to develop clear action points as you begin to reimagine your own educational settings.

Spend some time reflecting on your own educational experience.

What did LGBT+ inclusion, or exclusion, look like in your schooling?

Reflect on how your own views of education may have been shaped by those experiences.

Do you have certain views of what educational spaces should be like?

Reflect on the educational spaces you occupy now.

What do you feel you can or can't say about LGBT+ lives in your school? What knowledge and skills do you need to develop further to become more confident with LGBT+ inclusion?

PODCAST EPISODES REFERENCED IN THIS CHAPTER

- Season 2, Episode 13 – Professor Paul Baker

Paul (he/him) is a Professor of English Language and a researcher and writer. Paul joins us to discuss his latest book: *Outrageous!*, which charts the story of Section 28 and the battle for LGBT+ education.

- Season 2, Episode 1 – Professor Emeritus Sue Sanders & Lynne Nicholls

Sue (she/her) is an inspirational educator and the co-founder of LGBT+ History Month. Lynne (she/her) is the Chair of Trustees for charity Schools Out. They join us to discuss the history of LGBT+ inclusive education, LGBT+ History Month, and the work of Schools Out.

- Season 2, Episode 2 – Helen Richardson

Helen Richardson (she/her) is a Deputy Headteacher and led the diversity network for her school's Trust. Helen joins us to share her experience growing up during Section 28, and now working as an out, lesbian educator.

- Season 1, Episode 13 – Troy Jenkinson

Troy (he/him) is a primary school headteacher and children's book author. He joins us to share his experience as an early career teacher during Section 28, and now as an inclusive leader.

- Season 2, Episode 6 – Professor Catherine Lee

Catherine (she/her) was a PE teacher before stepping into academia at Anglia Ruskin University. She joins us to discuss her experience as a lesbian PE teacher during Section 28, her current research into LGBT+ leadership, and setting up the Courageous Leaders programme.

- Season 1, Episode 5 – B Guerriero

B (they/them) is a primary school teacher, LGBT+ youth worker, and a trustee of the UK Literacy Association. They join us to share their experience as a non-binary immigrant navigating a career in education.

- Season 1, Episode 6 – Karan Bhumbla

Karan (he/him) is a secondary school science teacher. He joins us to share his experience as a gay, Indian science teacher working to be a positive representation for all facets of his identity.

- Season 1, Episode 15 – Scotty Cartwright

Scotty (he/him) is an early career English teacher, who was a trainee when we spoke. He joins us to discuss his experience as a gay man joining the teaching profession.

REFERENCES

Anderson, Eric. (2010). *Inclusive Masculinity: The Changing Nature of Masculinities.* Routledge.

Baker, P. (2022). *Outrageous!: The Story of Section 28 and Britain's Battle for LGBT Education.* Reaktion Books.

Bradlow, J., Bartram, F., Guasp, A., & Jadva, V. (2017). *School Report.* Stonewall. www.stonewall.org.uk/resources/school-report-2017

Braun, Annette. (2011). 'Walking yourself around as a teacher': Gender and embodiment in student teachers' working lives. *British Journal of Sociology of Education, 32* (2), pp. 275–291. https://doi.org/10.1080/01425692.2011.547311

Brett, Adam. (2021). Changing the Narrative: A Photo Elicitation Study of LGBT Secondary School Teachers in England. Nottingham Trent University, UK.

Connell, Catherine. (2015). *School's Out; Gay and Lesbian Teachers in the Classroom* (1st ed.). University of California Press. www.jstor.org/stable/10.1525/j.ctt9qh2tp

DePalma, Renée and Elizabeth Atkinson. (2006). The sound of silence: Talking about sexual orientation and schooling. *Sex Education, 6* (4), pp. 333–349. https://doi.org/10.1080/14681810600981848

Department for Education. (2019). *Relationships Education, Relationships and Sex Education (RSE) and Health Education.*

Department for Education. (2022). *Keeping Children Safe in Education 2022. Statutory guidance for schools and colleges.*

Just Like Us. (2021). *Growing Up LGBT+: The Impact of School, Home and Coronavirus on LGBT+ Young People*. www.justlikeus.org/wp-content/uploads/2021/11/Just-Like-Us-2021-report-Growing-Up-LGBT.pdf

Lee, C. (2023). *Pretended: Schools and Section 28: Historical, Cultural and Personal Perspectives*. John Catt.

Pearce, N. E., Taylor, A., Park, C., Bryson, E., Clery, J. Curtice, & M. Phillips. (2013). *British Social Attitudes: The 30th Report.*

2

HETERONORMATIVITY

> *'This is not pretend. This is not make believe. This is reality, and that is fine, and great, and lawful – and there is nothing wrong with that. We should celebrate it like we would celebrate any other family type.'*
>
> *Allison Zionts*

IN THEORY

Heteronormativity is a crucial concept when discussing how to make spaces more LGBT+ inclusive. It is incredibly powerful, yet invisible, which frustratingly means it is simultaneously everywhere and nowhere. And its greatest trick? It allows heterosexual people to discuss their partners or romantic lives without being seen as discussing sexuality. LGBT+ people discussing their partner or lifestyle, on the other hand, can be seen as bringing inappropriate discussions of sex or sexuality into school... now, that is quite a trick.

So, what is this all-powerful heteronormativity? It's a concept that many people may not have heard of before, but it is an important one, possibly the most important one, that we need to get to grips with to create safe and inclusive school environments. Heteronormativity is the default and silent assumption that people are heterosexual. It may sound simple, or not even particularly surprising, but if you're an LGBT+ person, you know how isolating and exclusionary heteronormative spaces can be. Having something assumed of you means you are immediately burdened with the choice of whether to address the inaccurate assumption, leaving the other person feeling uncomfortable, or let the person believe something untrue about you, leaving you to absorb the discomfort. Having this feeling even once is distressing, but to have it regularly, can lead to negative mental health outcomes and the internalisation of shame.

I've lost count of the times in my career that I've had these questions asked of me. On my very first day as a qualified teacher, I remember sitting in the staff room, excited to start my new career. It was the first day of term, so staff were engaging in small talk and discussing what they had done during the summer holidays with their families and spouses. During the conversation, my head of department turned to me and asked whether I was married. It's important to say that my head of department was lovely and was no doubt just trying to include me in the conversation with this seemingly innocuous question. However, given that gay marriage wasn't legal at the time, what they were really asking me in front of the entire staff room was whether I had a wife. My mind went into overdrive as I created a mental decision tree of all the possible appropriate responses, trying to decide what the best thing would be to say in this setting. Did I just say no? It would be entirely true. Did I say no, but I was gay? Did I say I had a boyfriend? Did I say I would like to get married, but it isn't allowed? Starting a new job is stressful enough without having to think about which parts of your identity it is safe to reveal.

In the end, my blind panic took over and I just laughed and said 'no', and the issue was never raised again. I then felt unable to address my sexuality with the head of department as I didn't want to make them uncomfortable about their assumption, which sadly went on for several years. Using 'friend' when I was really talking about my boyfriend and concealing key parts of my identity all clouded the start of my career due to this heteronormative assumption on the first day. I look back now and wonder if I would have been comfortable enough to be honest if my head of department had simply changed their question from 'are you married?' to 'have you got a partner?' It's tough to answer that now, but it would at least have removed the loaded assumption, and signalled to me that this was a space where being something other than heterosexual might just be okay. This is just one small example, but I hope it highlights what heteronormativity can look and feel like for LGBT+ people. Now let's briefly explore the literature.

> Heteronormativity is defined as a system of valuing heterosexuality as the natural and normative sexual orientation, thereby devaluing all other expressions of sexuality, gender, and ways of family life (Page & Peacock 2013).

Page and Peacock's description of heterosexuality being valued as 'normative' and 'natural' illustrates how it is then possible to position non-heterosexual identities as abnormal, or worse, unnatural. Like much LGBT+ language, contemporary definitions of heteronormativity have evolved significantly from their early uses. Initially considered in the second wave of feminist theory (Rubin 1975) to explain how hierarchies were created to exploit women for the betterment of men, contemporary understandings of heteronormativity have developed with reference to sexuality, civil rights and what it means to be a good sexual citizen (Seidman 2001), which we'll explore shortly. Although uses of heteronormativity continue to evolve, it is possible to follow Rubin's line of reasoning that, from a feminist perspective, where men (and masculinity) were once favoured and economically advantaged by the suppression of women (and femininity), sexual identities or behaviours that did not conform to this rigid hierarchy would also be suppressed.

Jackson (2006) suggests that a contemporary definition of heteronormativity needs to include Rich's (1980) consideration of what she calls 'compulsory heterosexuality'; that institutionalised, normative heterosexuality regulates those kept within its boundaries as well as marginalising and sanctioning those outside of them. Jackson's (2006) consideration of heteronormativity highlights an important point, one that is really quite useful when trying to get schools to understand the significance of this work – that it is not simply LGBT+ people that are affected by heteronormativity – all people are. Not only does heteronormativity marginalise LGBT+ people, but it also constrains heterosexual people within a narrow set of normative expectations of what it is to be a good sexual citizen. Building upon Seidman's (2001) description, the good sexual citizen should therefore be gender conventional (explored in the next chapter), link sex to monogamous love and a marriage-like relationship, and defend family values. We could extend this further to include Turner's (2008) description of reproductive citizenship, where reproduction is seen as the ultimate form of citizenship. If this all sounds a bit wordy, I can guarantee you will have experienced or seen examples of this – just think about the kinds of things you hear in the staff room, and what is valued. I have heterosexual female friends in their 40s who are single, or married without children, who regularly experience microaggressions (a concept we'll define in Chapter 4) linked to their lack of childbearing: 'were you unable to have children?'; 'there's still time'; 'you'd make a great mum'; 'having children was the best thing that ever happened to me'.

If we think about it, heteronormativity is less about sexuality, and more about privileging a set of normative practices and ideals; a critique that has given rise to the concept of homonormativity. Homonormativity suggests that LGBT+ people can assimilate into heterosexual society by enacting these privileged ideals. We could also argue that heterosexual people can be excluded in society by not conforming to these ideals, as illustrated in the previous examples. As a gay, white, middle-class, cisgender male in a monogamous relationship, I carry a lot of privilege and tend not to be seen as particularly remarkable in educational settings. It is here that we need to consider intersectionality (discussed in Chapter 7) and employ some nuance when examining who is most greatly marginalised and damaged by heteronormativity. Unpacking the LGBT+ initialism is a useful starting point.

There are times when being seen as a homogenous LGBT+ community can have social and political benefits, but the critique that the gay rights movement focussed too heavily on gay, white men is a fair one. Homonormativity means that some LGBT+ identities are gaining greater acceptance in society, which should be cause for celebration, but in reality, means that other LGBT+ identities become further marginalised. We only need to think about the tropes that continue to be associated with bisexuality to understand that sexual identities that challenge binaries or don't conform to homonormative ideals continue to be seen as problematic.

Heteronormativity is a destructive force, one that doesn't really seem to benefit anyone: it's remarkable it has caught on in the way that it has! I jest of course, but at the start of the chapter I said that heteronormativity was one of the most important concepts for us to understand to create more inclusive spaces, and in naming it, we're off to a pretty good start. There is great power in naming things. In naming something, we make it real and valid; therefore, opening it up to critique. Through language, we can describe, expose, and change social reality and social constructs. Heteronormativity is a social construct, one that is held in the collective minds of people and requires continuous consent to exist. Like many social norms, heteronormativity remains invisible and is only revealed as a norm when something challenges it. For example, if I walked through the city centre holding my partner's hand, I would almost certainly receive homophobic comments (or at the very least some stares).

The good news about socially constructed ideas is that if we withdraw consent, they begin to lose their power, and it becomes possible to disrupt and challenge their dominance. I like to think of heteronormativity like the film *The Matrix*. In *The Matrix*, citizens are plugged into a program that continuously constructs a world made from code which is believed to be real. It's only once they have become unplugged and The Matrix has been named as an oppressive artificial tool, that they can see the systems that caged them. In the same way, by developing a critical awareness and language in our schools about the systems and structures that continue to produce heteronormativity, we can begin to disrupt its production.

To continue The Matrix analogy, it is helpful to consider exactly what the 'code' is that constructs schools as heteronormative spaces. We learnt in the last chapter about the silence and fear that Section 28 created, ensuring schools became places of self-policing where only heterosexuality remained visible. But two decades after its repeal, the heteronormative code continues to be produced in myriad ways: through the curriculums we teach; limited understandings of LGBT+ language; the cultures and ethos of schools; the fear of parental backlash; faith schools; the conflation of sex and sexuality; moral panic in the media; the list goes on. The passage of time alone does not undo the terrible damage of Section 28 – active change is required, after all, diversity is a fact, but inclusion is a choice. Schools are stubbornly heteronormative environments and need to be questioned and challenged at all levels to become more inclusive spaces.

If heteronormativity continues to constrain those within it, and marginalise those outside of it, then maybe it's time we got rid of it. We hope the later chapters will empower you with language, examples, strategies and confidence for you to begin challenging heteronormativity in your schools. If the stories from the podcast have taught us one thing, it's that it only takes a few people to make a big difference!

IN PRACTICE

Adam describes heteronormativity as powerful, yet invisible – as everywhere, yet nowhere. It reminds me of the old joke where one fish turns to another fish, and asks 'how's the water?' The other fish replies, 'what the hell is water?'

Okay… so it isn't a great joke, but it is a great metaphor for heteronormativity.

A fish doesn't know it's in water. It is surrounded by it, and always has been. It was raised in that environment and knows nothing else. Of course, as humans, we would know instantly if we found ourselves under water, because we can't breathe in that environment. Similarly, we are all raised in heteronormativity and many people don't realise they are surrounded by it – unless of course, they can't breathe in it.

That is how I felt as a young person in school.

From my earliest memories of being in school I felt different. I couldn't name my difference, but it was there, and it felt like it was growing. People around me began expecting me to be things that I was not, and to want things that I didn't. This subtle, but constant, messaging in my school told me that I was different, and that my difference was something I should be ashamed of. I didn't fit into my environment; as I got older, I began to feel like I was drowning in it. There were countless moments I felt like I couldn't breathe.

When a person can't breathe underwater, what do they do? Either they leave to find somewhere they can, or they exhaust themselves by constantly having to come up for air. Either way – intentionally or not – we cannot let this happen in our schools. As educators, we don't want any person (be that a student, a parent, or a colleague) to feel as though they can't breathe. Nobody should feel like they are drowning.

To prevent this from happening we need to understand heteronormativity, and to name it when we see it. It is all around us, even in our most basic understanding of the world. Often, we hear arguments about heterosexuality being 'natural', with the suggestion that anything else is therefore 'unnatural'. People use the animal kingdom as justification, so many of us come to believe that the natural world is heterosexual. This is incorrect.

David Lowbridge-Ellis (S2, E11) is a headteacher, writer, and the creator of the brilliant queer knowledge organiser. David created the knowledge organiser to collate lots of the queer knowledge he wishes he had been taught when he was in school. In our conversation with David he explains how important it was to include a section in his knowledge organiser which demonstrates queerness in the animal kingdom. There is a long list of species which scientists have observed displaying homosexual behaviours including examples of mammals, birds, fish, reptiles, amphibians, and insects. His knowledge organiser states clearly: humans aren't the only queer animals.

If heteronormativity lives in our basic understanding of the natural world, it can of course also stretch into our schools. Allison Zionts (S1, E3) is a secondary school teacher and PhD student, who explores heteronormativity within her research. She defines it as 'the concept, or reality, that the world is set up to make everything easier for heterosexual people'. Allison neatly talks us through several examples of how this materialises in our schools. She explains that in many schools, before a family even enters, they're often given a form which asks for the father's name and mother's name. The heterosexual assumption being clear before school life even begins. Allison talks about the books we read with our young people, the families we use in maths word problems, or the visuals around our school. If all we show are heterosexual people, then we risk teaching students these are the only types of relationships which are allowed. Allison encourages us to question our schools, and to consider what our young people will see and experience that might reinforce the idea that the only family types are men and women together. She gives examples of places to look: forms, policies, displays, book choices, and curriculum.

Often heteronormativity is subtle, and the changes Allison suggests in her episode can impact the subtle messaging our schools send to young people. However, heteronormativity can be more direct. Dominic Arnall (S1, E4) was the CEO of LGBT+ young people's charity 'Just Like Us' at the time we interviewed him. He tells us of LGBT+ teachers he has encountered who have been explicitly told by leadership that they cannot come out in school. Dominic suggests if this happened in other professions, it would result in legal action, yet we see it too often in our schools.

Of course, there are schools where the leadership are directly challenging heteronormativity and creating a space where everybody can be themselves. One of these leaders is the Deputy CEO Kyrstie Stubbs (S1, E8), who was a headteacher at the time we spoke with her. Kyrstie's episode is a masterclass in inclusive leadership, and she gives many examples of how to disrupt heteronormativity. Kyrstie tells us about an occasion when she was interviewing for a new teacher in her school. During the interview, Kyrstie asked one candidate about her home life to try and make her feel more comfortable, and to build up a conversation. The candidate told Kyrstie that she lived with her girlfriend. 'Oh, and where are you living?', Kyrstie replied. The candidate later told Kyrstie that she was so shocked by how Kyrstie had usualised (a word we will explore further in Chapter 5) her relationship. She explained how in previous schools revealing that information had led to her being bullied, and she couldn't believe how accepting Kyrstie had been.

Creating accepting schools like Kyrstie does benefits us all, and disrupting heteronormativity is part of that process. When we create a space where the permission to be yourself isn't dependent on your sexuality, then we free LGBT+ teachers to put all of their energy into being the best teacher they can be. Dr Shaun Dellenty (S2, E3) is a multi-award-winning teacher, LGBT+ inclusion advocate, trainer, inspirational speaker, and author. Shaun has been named one of the 100 most influential LGBT+ people in the UK and has achieved so much for our community. However, in our conversation Shaun tells us how much he was limited until he came out in his school in 2009. He describes having to waste around a fifth of his energy lying, covering up, changing pronouns, and concealing his identity. Just like Troy and Catherine in Chapter 1, his energy was wasted in concealing his identity. In response to a data set revealing homophobic bullying in his school, Shaun chose to come out in an assembly. He describes the response as joyful, but when he got home that evening, he cried for hours. His tears were tears of relief. Shaun tells us how freeing it was to finally be himself at work, and how powerful it was to now put all of the energy he had wasted concealing his identity into doing a good job.

Shaun shares a brilliant starting point to disrupting heteronormativity within a school. When delivering training, Shaun often asks, 'where, when and how did you first learn about heterosexual people and their lives, relationships and histories at school?' This question helps people to see what has always been invisible to them. This reflection helps us to see the water we have always been immersed in. Through reflecting on this question, people realise how heterosexuality has been promoted to them both subtly and directly.

Reflective conversations can be a great way to begin naming heteronormativity in your school, and this doesn't have to stop in the staff room. Eilidh Vizard (S1, E11) is a secondary science teacher who is passionate about representing both women and LGBT+ people in STEM (science, technology, engineering, and maths) subjects. Our conversation explored the importance of vocabulary, and she told us about how she has introduced heteronormativity to class discussion, breaking down what the word means and unpicking it as a group. In naming it, and discussing it, Eilidh plants a seed of questioning in her classroom which begins to disrupt the production of heteronormativity.

Through sharing these stories of heteronormativity in practice, I hope we have gone some way in making the invisible, visible to you. Having heard these stories, you should now be in a better position to notice, name, and challenge heteronormativity in your own educational settings.

The natural next step after noticing and naming problems in our schools is to begin working to solve these problems. Thus far, we have presented two problems, but have not yet provided the much-needed solutions to them.

Let me reassure you – the solutions are coming. But we must have a full understanding of the problems we face before we begin to navigate the possible solutions. Before we can explore the ways to reimagine our educational spaces and unroot silence and shame from our schools, we have one final problem to introduce you to: cisnormativity.

IN ACTION

Spend some time reflecting on the educational spaces you occupy.

How do you see heteronormativity within those spaces?

Reflect on the language you use, and the language you hear in your educational space.

How might that language promote heteronormativity?

Reflect on where there is room for change in your practice.

What small changes could begin to disrupt heteronormativity in your educational spaces?

PODCAST EPISODES REFERENCED IN THIS CHAPTER

- Season 2, Episode 11 – David Lowbridge-Ellis

David (he/they) is a headteacher, writer and trainer. He joins us to share brilliant tips on how to make educational spaces more inclusive, and how to be an effective and authentic leader.

- Season 1, Episode 3 – Allison Zionts

Allison (she/her) is a secondary school teacher and PhD researcher exploring LGBTQ+ safe spaces. She joins us to discuss her research, and share her experience as a bisexual, Jewish woman.

- Season 1, Episode 4 – Dominic Arnall

Dominic (he/him) was the CEO of LGBT+ young people's charity 'Just Like Us' at the time we spoke. He joins us to discuss the great work that Just Like Us does to support LGBT+ young people and schools.

- Season 1, Episode 8 – Kyrstie Stubbs

Kyrstie (she/her) is an inspirational former headteacher, now Deputy CEO, and an LGBT+ ally. She joins us to share how her leadership approaches diversity, equity, and inclusion in a holistic, and meaningful way.

- Season 2, Episode 3 – Dr Shaun Dellenty

Shaun (he/him) is a multi-award-winning educator, LGBT+ inclusion advocate, trainer, inspirational speaker, and author. He joins us to share his experience as a gay primary school teacher, now supporting LGBT+ inclusion through training and consultancy.

- Season 1, Episode 11 – Eilidh Vizard

Eilidh (she/her) is a secondary school science teacher. She joins us to discuss inclusive language, and representation for LGBT+ people, and women in STEM.

REFERENCES

Jackson, S. (2006). Interchanges: Gender, sexuality and heterosexuality: The complexity (and limits) of heteronormativity. *Feminist Theory, 7*(1), pp. 105–121. 10.1177/1464700106061462

Page, A. D., & Peacock, J. R. (2013). Negotiating identities in a heteronormative context. *Journal of Homosexuality, 60*(4), pp. 639–654. 10.1080/00918369.2012.724632

Rich, A. (1980). Compulsory heterosexuality and lesbian existence. *Signs: Journal of Women in Culture and Society, 5*(4), pp. 631–660. 10.1086/493756

Rubin, G. (1975). The traffic in women: Notes on the 'political economy' of sex. In R. R. Reiter (Ed.), *Toward an Anthropology of Women* (pp. 157–210). Monthly Review Press.

Seidman, S. (2001). From identity to queer politics: Shifts in normative heterosexuality and the meaning of citizenship. *Citizenship Studies, 5*(3), pp. 321–328. 10.1080/13621020120085270

Turner, B. S. (2008). Citizenship, reproduction and the state: International marriage and human rights AU. *Citizenship Studies, 12*(1), pp. 45–54. 10.1080/1362102 0701794166

3

CISNORMATIVITY

'I've had more than one child on numerous occasions ask me, but can you actually be a transgender RE teacher, or Catholic and transgender?'

George White

IN THEORY

In the last chapter, we discussed the importance of identifying and challenging heteronormativity to develop more inclusive spaces for all. However, heteronormativity only relates to sexuality; to make schools fully LGBT+ inclusive, we also need to examine the roles of sex and gender. To help us do this, we are going to welcome to the stage heteronormativity's equally unhelpful sibling, cisnormativity.

Much like heteronormativity, cisnormativity is the assumption that all people are cisgender, meaning their gender identity aligns with the sex they were assigned at birth. There is a lot to unpack in this sentence alone, especially when trying to understand the distinct differences between sex and gender. In this chapter, we will try to develop a nuanced distinction between the two, before examining them within the context of schools. It is important to note that whilst the definitions of sex and gender we share are our own, they are inline with the definitions held at the time of publishing by the UK Government, the NHS, the ONS, the WHO, and all major LGBTQ+ charities.

It would probably be helpful here to remind ourselves that although the LGBT+ initialism is ubiquitously used, it is in fact describing three distinct and separate aspects:

sexuality, gender, and sex. While there are times it makes sense to discuss these collectively, to make our schools more inclusive we need to interrogate these aspects individually. It is common for sexuality and gender to be conflated, but it's important for us to remember they are indeed separate. You could be a cisgender gay, straight, or bisexual person, in the same way you could be a transgender gay, straight or bisexual person.

Before we grapple with the complicated business of gender, let's begin by trying to define what we mean by sex – the thing we are assigned at birth. Sex is generally defined as a combination of sexual organs, chromosomes, and hormones most commonly categorised within the binary of male or female. Although this feels like a neat categorisation, it isn't, and these physical and biological features vary widely from person to person. The fact that I'm a 39-year-old who can't grow a beard yet teach teenagers with facial hair a pirate would be proud of, painfully illustrates this point. To further complicate things, if we accept the holistic definition of intersex, it is estimated that up to 1.7% of the population are intersex (Fausto-Sterling 2006) and therefore have variations in their sex characteristics that are different from society's expectations of 'male' or 'female' bodies.

You might be thinking, hang on, this explanation is making me less clear about the definition of sex! Don't worry, this is a good thing. When thinking about sex and gender, we need to come out of our comfort zones and challenge our binary thinking. So yes, while people are assigned either male or female at birth (in most countries, even if they are intersex), within each of these categories exists wide and wonderful variation.

Sex, then, is our biological features – this is a useful distinction to help us understand how it differs from gender.

We all have a different relationship with gender, making it a complicated and personal topic; something we need to be sensitive of when doing this work. In discussing gender, we also need to locate it in both space and time, as gender is a concept that has meant different things historically and means different things throughout the world; for example, some cultures have for a long time recognised more than two genders. Our discussions of gender, therefore, need to be positioned as ones that are Western and present day, recognising the language and ideas we use to discuss gender could differ from ones used as little as 10 years ago. Appreciating that understandings of gender vary so greatly highlights the fact that gender is a socially constructed, nuanced and continuously evolving concept.

A good way to describe gender, then, is as a set of socially constructed ideas that are mapped on top of sex. It's hard to recognise that gender is socially constructed and not something natural or permanent, or even linked to sex. It's no surprise – we are conflating sex with gender from the moment we are born. Think about it, what's the first question people ask when a baby is born, usually 'is it a boy or a girl?'. It's bizarre when you think about it – what does it matter at that stage? But people are desperate to know as it allows them to calibrate their relationship to the child and decide whether to buy the blue dinosaur onesie or the pink princess dress, and understand how they should communicate and play with the child. There have been various studies exploring the ways in which adults subconsciously change their behaviour to speak and interact with children based upon the sex the child is assumed to be. I recommend reading the results of the famous 'Baby x' study (Seavey, Katz, & Zalk 1975) to appreciate the ways in which babies and children subtly begin to learn about gender and how it should be 'performed'.

Judith Butler is a leading gender scholar and identifies the ways in which gender is constructed through what they call gender performativity. Butler argues that often gender isn't something we are, it is something we do. Considering gender as a verb, and not a noun, allows us to conceptualise the ways in which gender is constructed through the performativity of the things we do, the ways we speak, the clothes we wear, and the movements of our body.

> Gender is an identity tenuously constituted in time, instituted in an exterior space through a stylized repetition of acts. The effect of gender is produced through the stylization of the body and, hence, must be understood as the mundane way in which bodily gestures, movements, and styles of various kinds constitute the illusion of an abiding gender.
>
> (Butler 2006)

Gender, Butler argues, is something that continues to be produced and reproduced through time. Analysing this in the context of schools, we can begin to see the ways in which children are 'taught' gender through both the formal and hidden curriculum. Think about some of the ways in which schools communicate information about gender to children: uniform policies; sports; toilets; groupings; activities; language; to name but a few. (This is a good task to use if you ever deliver CPD in your school – I often get colleagues to write their suggestions on post-its. It is always striking when the results are collated, and staff see the huge number of ways in which gender is communicated.)

As argued in the previous chapter, the good thing about socially constructed ideas is that their production can be interrupted. If we think of gender as something that is implicitly taught to children, then we as teachers have a huge role to play in challenging gender stereotypes and providing inclusive alternatives. While there are gendered aspects of school we may not be able to change on an individual level, such as toilets, considering the language we use is a small thing we can all do that can have a huge impact.

Language constructs reality, and as such, the language we use with our students and colleagues is crucial. As we can't think outside of language, we often need a new vocabulary and set of ideas to help us imagine an alternative to the existing conditions. Spend a moment thinking about the way students are usually addressed in class – 'ladies and gents' or 'boys and girls' being fairly universal examples. This may not sound like pernicious language, but it does drip feed a message of an expected binary, which if you were non-binary or questioning your gender, could be distressing. This could be further distressing in single sex schools or lessons such as PE if your whole group were addressed as their assumed gender, 'okay girls...', 'right boys...'.

I really enjoy hearing the creative ways in which teachers are changing the language they use to be more inclusive and less focussed on gender. My favourite examples are from educators who address their students as the discipline they are within that lesson, for example, 'morning physicists'; 'let's get started geographers'; 'great work mathematicians' – aren't these wonderful! Students are not just being reduced to their gender, but they are being empowered with scholarly language which might just allow them to picture themselves as future historians, musicians, or linguists.

As a business teacher, I haven't quite settled on what to call my students (please tweet me your suggestions), but I did recently try calling a group 'entrepreneurs'. What started as a bit of fun actually turned into an important moment to challenge cisnormativity that got my students to think about the importance of language. When addressing whole classes I usually use 'folks' or their year group, e.g., 'Year 10'. When I started experimenting with 'entrepreneurs', one of my Year 11s asked why I was using the term, or to quote them exactly, 'erm, Sir, why are you calling us that, it's weird'. I explained that there aren't many gender-neutral collective terms, and after they stared at me blankly for a few seconds, we had a brilliant discussion about language and what it conveys. The next lesson, I couldn't believe it when a group of students came in and told me they'd been thinking about what I had said, before presenting me with a list of collective terms I could also use (my favourite being peeps!). This conversation had a huge impact in getting students to think about the significance of language and the small things we can all do to be more inclusive. It also had ripple effects in the wider school as the students went on to have conversations with other teachers which then inspired fantastic lunchtime conversations in the staff room.

This story highlights the simple ways in which cisnormativity can be gently challenged. Through calling into question 'the way things have always been done', we begin to develop a critical awareness in ourselves and those around us, allowing us to imagine the educational spaces that we would like, rather than the ones we have inherited.

It's important to acknowledge that the current discourse surrounding gender and trans rights is divisive and often toxic. Imagine if you were a trans child or teenager now and saw your identity being debated and demeaned within the media on a daily basis. It is vital for this reason that we are creating spaces in our schools for these students, where they can feel safe and where their identities are validated. We need to create positive narratives for our students and ensure they have role models to look up to.

Making schools safer spaces for trans and gender-questioning students isn't always easy and an argument that often arises is that us 'woke' people are trying to erase the categories 'man' and 'woman'. This is obviously not the case, but understanding and acknowledging concerns is an important step in making progress and bringing people with us. As I said earlier, people's identity is very important to them, and no one is suggesting these are removed from schools. We are simply trying to create safe spaces where gender is not assumed or expected.

We said in the last chapter that heteronormativity restricts and restrains all people, and the same could be said for cisnormativity. Gendered expectations of what men and women are able to do are unbelievably limiting, and I bet we can all point to times in our life where we've felt restricted by gender expectations ('boys don't cry'; 'that's not very lady-like'). In calling gender into question and removing unhelpful or outdated assumptions, we can create educational spaces where people don't feel constrained or limited by what is expected of them; spaces where people feel free and safe to explore their relationship with gender.

IN PRACTICE

At the beginning of my teaching career, I worked with a brilliant educator called Tom Wallace. During training one day, Tom showed me a video which I still think about years later. The video was called The Backwards Brain Cycle, posted by Smarter Every Day on YouTube. In the video we meet Destin, a keen cyclist who learnt to ride a bike at a young age. We've all heard people describe something as like riding a bike, the idea being that once you have learnt to ride a bike it is something you can never forget, right?

Not in this video. The story begins with Destin being presented with a backwards bike: a bike where the handlebars have the opposite reaction to that of a usual bike – if you steer left, the bike will instead turn right. As you can imagine, Destin's first attempt to ride the backwards bike does not go well. Neither does his second, or his third. In fact, it takes Destin eight months of gently trying every day to finally learn how to ride the backwards bike.

Why does it take Destin so long to learn how to ride a new bike – something he had always known how to do? It's obvious – Destin isn't just learning; this task requires him to be simultaneously unlearning. Every day, as Destin picked up the backwards bike, he was learning something new while having to unlearn everything he had been taught his entire life about how to ride a bike.

In reading Adam's explanation of sex and gender, maybe you experienced the challenge of learning and unlearning. As Adam suggested, we were raised into a particular understanding of sex, gender, and gender roles – to unlearn some of this can be challenging.

So, let me be clear – nobody is born with gender literacy. Adam, I, and the guests who you will hear from in this chapter have all had to go through a process of learning and unlearning to get to the understanding we have now.

When I started learning about gender, I had to unlearn the misconception that gender identity was a new thing. I read about the rich, long history of gender diverse people. While the language used around gender identity is new and developing, gender diverse people are not a new phenomenon. In our conversation with Karan Bhumbla (S1, E6) he tells us about the hijra, who are third gender people with cultural significance in India. Hijra people are neither man nor women, and there are many more examples like this of gender diversity across the globe, and through history.

The most meaningful way I supported my own process of learning and unlearning gender was to listen to the lived experiences of trans people and explore how a cisnormative system impacts them. Over the next few pages, you are going to meet B, Claire, and George – all brilliant educators, guests on our podcast, and trans people.

B Guerriero (S1, E5) is an experienced primary school teacher and LGBT+ youth worker. We met them briefly in Chapter 1 when discussing their upbringing in Italy. They are non-binary, which they define for us:

> 'I am transgender, which means that my gender identity doesn't match with what is written on my birth certificate. I specifically identify as non-binary, which means that my gender identity is not female and it is not male. I am somewhere

> in between, not really sure where. I think it is worth mentioning that gender is a spectrum, there is no one way of being a non-binary person as much as there is no one way of being a male or a female. I use gender-neutral pronouns, my pronouns are they and them, which means that when people refer to me they will say not say he or she is Italian, they would say they are Italian. I also use a gender-neutral title which is Mx.'

What a brilliant explanation! So clear and honest. We went on to discuss B's experiences as a non-binary person in education. B has a picture of their first day of school, 5 years old, standing next to a blackboard with the date written on it. In the picture, B tells us they are crying, tears which their mother put down to separation anxiety. In fact, B was crying because they felt so uncomfortable wearing the skirt that their mother had chosen for them.

For as long as B can remember, they have been questioning their gender identity. As a non-binary person, gendered nouns made it challenging for B to linguistically exist in Italy, and they later moved to England. Eventually settling in Manchester, B started to attend a networking group with other non-binary people. B was 26 when they met people who were like them for the first time.

Through the episode B tells us of challenges they face as a non-binary person: being misgendered in school; having no safe gender-neutral toilet to use; and being shouted at in the street. Whenever they enter a classroom, they await what they refer to as *the question*: 'are you a boy or a girl?'

B doesn't shy away from the question; they love it because they see it for what it is: an opportunity to begin an educational and empathetic conversation. Often, they draw a line on the board, with the words man and women at the end of the line. B explains that this is where most people are, but there are also some people who fall between or outside of this line, there are some people that aren't at the same point every day. This starts a powerful conversation about gender expectations of hair, clothes, hobbies and how our gender shouldn't limit these. As B so brilliantly summarises, 'there is a lot of growth just outside of understanding'.

It is strange for me to listen back to our conversation with B. Towards the end, I ask them, 'what would you say to a non-binary teacher who is just starting to think about having these conversations in school?' I posed the question as a hypothetical, but truthfully that hypothetical was my reality. I was just beginning to share my own non-binary identity at the time we held this conversation. B's advice on the podcast helped me to navigate that journey. They also advised all teachers on how they can begin to challenge cisnormativity. They encourage us all to show in our classrooms, displays, and book choices, that there is more than just cisgender people. Make it visible, they suggest, plan specifically for inclusive education. Be curious, ask questions, but be respectful as you explore.

Some of B's life experiences are well conceptualised in a separate conversation with Claire Birkenshaw (S1, E9). Claire worked as a senior leader in secondary education before becoming a senior lecturer at Leeds Beckett University. She is an incredible academic thinker, and a trans woman. Throughout our conversation, Claire talks us through her thoughts on how hetero/cisnormativity impacts LGBT+ people.

Claire points out, as Adam discussed earlier, that the first question asked when a child is born is 'are they a boy or girl?' Often before asking if the child is healthy, or how the family is doing. From the moment a child is born, they are placed on what Claire calls the 'cisnormative trajectory'. She explains how this trajectory can force LGBT+ people to contain themselves. While heterosexual, cisgendered teenagers have societal permission to explore themselves and have milestone experiences, many young LGBT+ don't feel that they have that permission. Instead, they spend their formative years building scripts to read from, which aren't true to themselves, but help them to navigate a hetero/cisnormative space. Claire describes how LGBT+ young people often experience their formative years as a time of stasis, where they often have to put their identity exploration on hold until their 20s.

As they get older, they may begin to find certain spaces, or specific safe people, where they can begin to unfold and be more authentic – like the support group B attended in Manchester. Claire explains how this creates a repeated process of unfolding in certain spaces and folding back up in others. Picture a piece of paper in that repeated process – there are only so many times we can fold and unfold before those folds become rips and start to cause damage.

Claire tells us, as a trans person, she is often asked questions which would never be asked of a cisgender person. She suggests these questions are not about getting to know her or making her more comfortable. They are instead about trying to remove the other person's discomfort with her existence.

All these experiences are part of the cycle of cisnormativity, which Claire challenges us to disrupt. But she acknowledges that when we attempt to disrupt a system which has been a certain way for a long time, this can build anxiety. Sometimes, she argues, this change anxiety is projected onto parents or children and used by teachers as an excuse to avoid the disruption. But, if we aren't actively disrupting this cycle, then we are inactively perpetuating it. Claire explains how the scripts she mentioned earlier can help support this disruption and remove the anxiety it causes.

Having a script in place can help us to navigate difficult circumstances, but she suggests many educators do not have their scripts in place when it comes to LGBT+ inclusion. Without those scripts, or the confidence to deliver them, many resort to silence; the result of which we saw in our exploration of Section 28 in Chapter 1. Instead, Claire calls for the development of teacher knowledge, so they have prepared scripts to help navigate conversations around challenging heteronormativity and cisnormativity.

If we agree that further support is needed to build knowledge, scripts, and confidence around LGBT+ inclusion, a great place to look is in the work of educators who are already doing this so well. George White (S1, E2) is a special part of the Pride & Progress community because he was our very first guest! We recorded our first interview with George only days after deciding to go ahead with the project. As I unpacked my shiny new microphone and sent out the Zoom link, I was beginning to feel a little nervous. What if I'm terrible at hosting? What if I don't know what to ask? What if nobody listens? All my nerves were settled within minutes of meeting George. He is warm, kind, hilarious, and an outstanding educator. The story George shared with us that day remains one of the most powerful stories I have heard in education.

George started his teaching career as Miss White. He passed the first two terms of his NQT year but found himself struggling during his third term. George was having what he describes to us as an existential crisis of gender, and it was beginning to impact his work. His mentor noticed, and asked George why his standards seemed to be slipping. George knew he had to be honest. Taking a friend with him for support, he arranged a meeting and told his school that he is transgender. Knowing that transitioning in school might be challenging, George moved to a new school when he started to transition.

Except – it wasn't a new school, really. It was the school he used to attend himself as a student. George is now a trans man who teaches religious education in the same Catholic high school he attended as a young student being perceived as a woman.

George tells us, 'I've had more than one child on numerous occasions ask me, "but can you actually be a transgender RE teacher, or Catholic and transgender?" and I'm standing right in front of them – so of course, the answer is "yes"'. Throughout his career people have suggested that George should avoid any questions about his trans identity from pupils, giving him a general feeling that being quiet about being trans is seen as preferable. He disagrees. George explains that his cisgendered, heterosexual colleagues are empowered to talk openly about their partner, their children, or their life outside of school in a way which he has sometimes felt expected to be silent about. George is open about his gender identity in school, and in our conversation he shares suggestions of how others too can disrupt cisnormativity.

He wears a pronoun pin badge and signs his emails off with his name and pronouns. This helps to usualise conversations around pronouns and encourages people to not make assumptions around gender identity. He encourages all schools to look closely at their uniform policies or staff dress codes and ensure these make room for all people. Most importantly, George makes space for honest conversations about diversity and inclusion in his classroom. These small acts of visibility have allowed George to quietly, but quite powerfully, disrupt the cisnormative cycle in his school.

I started this chapter by acknowledging that there is much to learn and unlearn when we begin exploring gender. If this chapter is a lot of information for you, be assured that it was once new information for us all. Like Destin and his backwards bike, it takes time and practice to see things in a different way. Destin had to gently try every day, and so do we.

However, what I hope these stories have shown is the importance of committing to doing that work. I hope that hearing the lived experiences of trans and gender diverse people motivates you to gently try every day to learn and unlearn, finding new ways to improve our educational spaces and make them more inclusive for these people.

It can be easy to dismiss things which we don't fully understand yet, but in doing so, we dismiss the experiences of these people, and we give permission for cycles of discrimination to continue. If we say we don't understand, and we use that as an excuse to allow discrimination, then we contribute to the discomfort and discrimination LGBT+ people face.

Alok Vaid-Menon is a non-binary poet, performer and thinker who argues that too often the focus is placed on comprehension when it should be on compassion. Their argument is that we don't have to fully comprehend a person to have compassion with them. You don't have to fully understand, or agree, with everything we have presented in this chapter to support trans and gender diverse people. You can have compassion, with or without full comprehension.

So far in this book, we have explored the educational context, including the shadow of silence and shame caused by Section 28, and how hetero/cisnormativity operates in educational spaces to exclude LGBT+ people.

Now, having presented the problems, it is time to turn to exploring the solutions. In the following chapters, we will explore the solutions and themes we need to consider to continue reimagining, to continue unrooting silence and shame, and to finally create educational spaces which are truly LGBT+ inclusive.

IN ACTION

Spend some time reflecting on the educational spaces you occupy.

How do you see cisnormativity within those spaces?

Reflect on the language you use, and the language you hear in your educational space.

In what ways is that language binary, and how might this exclude some people?

Reflect on where there is room for change in your practice.

What small changes could begin to disrupt cisnormativity in your educational spaces? How do students learn about gender in your school, and do your physical spaces make room for all people?

PODCAST EPISODES REFERENCED IN THIS CHAPTER

- Season 1, Episode 6 – Karan Bhumbla

Karan (he/him) is a secondary school science teacher. He joins us to share his experience as a gay, Indian science teacher working to be positive representation for all facets of his identity.

- Season 1, Episode 5 – B Guerriero

B (they/them) is a primary school teacher, LGBT+ youth worker, and a trustee of the UK Literacy Association. They join us to share their experience as a non-binary immigrant navigating a career in education.

- Season 1, Episode 9 – Claire Birkenshaw

Claire (she/her) is a former headteacher, academic, and incredible thinker. She joins us to share her experience as a trans woman, and to conceptualise some of the experiences of LGBT+ people with theory and thinking.

- Season 1, Episode 2 – George White

George (he/him) is a teacher of Religious Education, inclusion leader, and LGBTQ+ inclusion consultant. He joins us to share his experience as a trans man now teaching in the same Catholic school he attended as a student.

REFERENCES

Butler, Judith. (2006). *Gender Trouble: Feminism and the Subversion of Identity.* Taylor & Francis Group. http://ebookcentral.proquest.com/lib/ntuuk/detail.action?docID=710077

Fausto-Sterling, Anne. (2006). The five sexes, revisited. In Maxine Baca Zinn, Pierrette Hondagneu-Sotelo and Michael A. Messne (Eds), *Gender through the Prism of Difference.* Oxford University Press.

National Health Service. (2021). *Sex, gender, and sexuality.* Retrieved from: https://service-manual.nhs.uk/content/inclusive-content/sex-gender-and-sexuality

Office for National Statistics. (2019). *What is the difference between sex and gender?* Retrieved from: https://www.ons.gov.uk/economy/environmentalaccounts/articles/whatisthedifferencebetweensexandgender/2019-02-21

Seavey, Carol A., Phyllis A. Katz, & Sue Rosenberg Zalk. (1975). Baby X. *Sex Roles, 1* (2), pp. 103–109.

Vaid-Menon, Alok. (2020). *Beyond the gender binary.* New York: Penguin

World Health Organisation. (N.A). *Gender and health.* Retrieved from: https://www.who.int/health-topics/gender#tab=tab_1

4

LANGUAGE

> *'When people use the right words I feel seen, and I feel safe. When people don't use the right words it can make me feel invisible.'*
>
> *A Non-binary Primary School Student*

IN THEORY

The chapters up to this point have explored three of the biggest barriers to greater LGBT+ inclusivity: our non-inclusive educational history, heteronormativity, and cisnormativity. Now the fun bit! We get to think about the ways we can challenge the status quo to make our classrooms truly inclusive spaces. We have already begun discussing one of the most impactful ways we can do this in the cisnormativity chapter – through the power of language.

Language really is a magical thing. Words give us the power of thought and the ability to imagine; they allow us to ponder, describe, evoke, feel, discuss, and create. Language is the artist's brush, the builder's tools; an instrument with which to alter consciousness. It is also the most important thing we can equip ourselves with to make our classrooms inclusive. There are so many times in my life I have learnt a word or encountered an idea for the first time that has altered my perspective or worldview. I couldn't get the idea of 'sonder' out of my head after I first heard it (the profound feeling of realising that everyone, including strangers passing in the street, has a life as complex as one's own, which they are constantly living despite one's personal lack of awareness of it... really helps put your own problems in perspective).

I also remember how important it felt to learn about microaggressions for the first time. It was so powerful to be able to describe and give a name to something I had experienced my entire life. We will return to microaggressions shortly.

The language available to both staff and students has the ability to either maintain or disrupt the existing conditions. Language that is either discriminatory or not overtly inclusive can continue the othering of LGBT+ identities, ensuring the dominance of cis/heteronormativity. As Pellegrini (1992) argues, language determines thought, meaning it is impossible to think outside of existing norms without the language and understanding to imagine an alternative. Ferfolja (2007) suggests that schools privilege certain groups and identities in society while marginalising others, reasoning the social order is legitimised through being couched in the language of 'normalcy' and 'common sense'.

Analysing the language used in schools can reveal how cis/heteronormativity is quietly held in place, without attracting claims of discrimination, using language that is implicitly considered 'normal'. By identifying and naming this language and its implicit meanings, norms can be challenged, making way for a culture and vocabulary that allows for norms to be questioned and alternatives to be imagined.

With that said, let us now return to microaggressions. Analysing the microaggressions used in schools can quickly reveal what is held as 'normal' and 'common sense'. Originally conceptualising forms of racism, microaggression theory has evolved to consider the types of exclusion members of different marginalised groups may experience. Microaggressions are defined as 'subtle forms of discrimination, often unconscious or unintentional, that communicate hostile or derogatory messages, particularly to and about members of historically marginalised social groups' (Nadal et al. 2016). The types of microaggressions that people may experience are further sub-categorised:

- Microassaults refer to explicit or purposeful comments or actions meant to demean the recipient, e.g., homophobic or abusive language, or even violence.
- Microinsults refer to unconscious verbal or non-verbal communication that can demean a person's identity, e.g., explicit boys and girls changing rooms or toilets may make a trans individual feel unsure/uncomfortable which to use and then implicitly feeling they don't belong in that environment, or teachers assuming boys like girls and vice versa through blanket statements.
- Microinvalidations which are also often unconscious and include communications that exclude, negate, or nullify the realities of individuals of oppressed groups (Sue et al. 2007), e.g., instances in which LGBT+ people are told that

their perceptions of discrimination are unfounded or nonsensical, or telling someone that has come out to you that you always knew or that it's not a big deal.

Microaggressions are small and subtle and, without critical awareness, often pass undetected. Marginalised people may experience examples of these every day, producing a death-by-a-thousand-paper-cuts effect. A colleague may think misgendering someone or their partner isn't a big deal, but when the sum of these comments weigh on the shoulders of the recipient, the burden becomes heavy and the shame internalised.

Naming something as a microaggression and encouraging people to reflect upon what they are conveying is an incredibly powerful tool. There is of course a time and place to do this, but I have delivered highly impactful training with both staff and students discussing microaggressions and the language we choose to use. Giving people time to think about the language they use often reveals subconscious values and views that they themselves are shocked to learn. Getting colleagues to reflect on their own biases and unconscious views is incredibly effective; after this type of training, people leave with a greater degree of self-awareness, and importantly, the determination to learn more and do better. As Rich (1994) describes, teachers need to understand the power of the language they use.

> When those who have the power to name and to socially construct reality choose not to see you or hear you... when someone with the authority of a teacher, say, describes the world and you are not in it, there is a moment of psychic disequilibrium, as if you looked in the mirror and saw nothing.
>
> (Rich 1994)

Giving staff and students time to think about the language they use and what it communicates is an important step in making schools LGBT+ inclusive. We also need to ensure people are comfortable using the language of the LGBT+ community. Language constructs reality, and so if we are not using the language LGBT+ people use themselves, we are at risk of invalidating or denying their reality and creating, as Rich describes, moments of psychic disequilibrium.

LGBT+ language is always evolving and changing, as is the initialism itself. We choose to use LGBT+, rather than LGBTQIA+ or similar versions, not to exclude other sexual and gender identities, but because continuing to add letters may be done so at the risk of overlooking other identities (it also becomes increasingly cumbersome to say). I prefer to think about the LGBT+ initialism as a collective umbrella for non-heterosexual and non-cisgender identities. Queer is a word that is sometimes used as an umbrella term in this way, too. Although we have included a brief glossary in the introduction, it would be useful to spend some time here exploring and defining the extended LGBTQIA+ initialism in more detail. I would caveat the following definitions by not only repeating that their uses evolve over time, but by also saying that people may use these terms differently. Whichever way someone chooses to describe their identity is real and valid and something we should of course respect, especially for young people who may be in an exploratory or transitional phase.

- Lesbian. A term to describe women who are attracted to women. Some women prefer to use gay rather than lesbian to describe themselves.
- Gay. A term that describes same sex attraction, traditionally men.
- Bisexual. A person who is attracted to men and women. Pansexual is a similar term which describes someone who is attracted to a person irrespective of gender, therefore including non-binary and genderqueer people.
- Trans. Trans, or transgender, refers to someone whose gender identity doesn't align with their sex assigned at birth. A person doesn't need to have received medical intervention to identify as a trans person or to receive rights under the Equalities Act (2010). While some people still identify as transexual, it is an increasingly outdated term that is sometimes used in a derogatory way and is best avoided.
- Intersex. A person who has variations in their primary and/or secondary sex characteristics that are different from society's expectations of 'male' or 'female' bodies (this may include sexual organs, chromosomes, or hormones). Intersex is discussed in more detail in the cisnormativity chapter.
- Queer. Queer can be used in a variety of ways and is a reclaimed slur. As previously described, queer can be an umbrella term; it can also be used as a term that seeks to disrupt or reject categorisation or identification. Queer theory is a discipline that interrogates our understandings and classifications of sexuality and gender and is a great way for us to examine the ways in which gender and sexuality are socially constructed. Meg-John Barker (2016) has written an excellent book called *Queer: A Graphic History* which explores queer and its many meanings and uses.
- Questioning. The Q can also be used for questioning and refers to someone who may be questioning their sexual or gender identity.
- Asexual/Aromantic. Someone who doesn't experience sexual/romantic desire.
- Non-binary. This is a term that is used in a variety of ways and it's important we take the lead of someone sharing their non-binary identity with us. Non-binary

often refers to someone who doesn't identify as either a man or women. It could also be that they experience gender as a spectrum – this could also be described as genderqueer. Non-binary people often use gender-neutral language such as they/them pronouns, or the title Mx (pronounced Mix or Mux). They may have other neutral titles and pronouns they prefer.
- The + refers to other non-heterosexual and non-cisgender identities. It recognises the many wonderful ways in which people can explore and describe their identity, as well as acknowledging that language continually changes and evolves.

We appreciate that this language can be unfamiliar and confusing for people, especially if they're not using it regularly. Having a glossary display in your school is a good way to keep this language in the forefront of people's minds. As part of my doctoral research, I saw a great piece of practice in a school that had a 'word of wonder' sign in every classroom. The word changed each week and below the word it said 'ask me [the teacher] what this means'. One week the word was heteronormativity, and the discussions and debates it generated were phenomenal! Teachers and students engaged in transformational conversations about what this word meant and what it looked and felt like. It empowered staff and students to reflect on their own practice and to identify things in school that had the potential to exclude.

Having a chance to practise and even script using LGBT+ inclusive language is also important. Sharing your pronouns or referring to a non-binary person as they/them can initially feel unfamiliar and can lead to people not using the correct language for fear of getting it wrong. Giving staff a chance to practise and script this language is helpful as it allows them to make mistakes in a safe space, develop their confidence in using it, and ask questions if they're unsure. I always start training sessions by asking people to share their name and pronouns if they are comfortable doing so. Although initially they can feel self-conscious, they quickly realise the importance of sharing pronouns and how they can use this in their classrooms to ensure they don't assume students' gender. Scripting is also useful, whether it's giving teachers a response they can use if a child comes out to them (Allison Zionts gives a great example in her episode) or showing how to apologise and move on if you make a mistake. LGBT+ people are more appreciative and understanding of someone who is trying to use their language but makes a mistake, compared to those who fear getting it wrong and don't use it at all.

Language has the power to include or exclude; to validate or demean; to maintain or disrupt. In developing a common language, schools can empower their staff and students to think critically and challenge what has been previously considered 'normal' or 'common sense'. With the right vocabulary and culture, we can disrupt the existing and speak new and inclusive realities into being.

IN PRACTICE

When I trained to be a primary school teacher, I was placed in a gorgeous school in the North West of England. My teaching career began in the hall of that school as I attended their first staff training day.

Thirty minutes in, and I was feeling confident. The school was easy to get to, the building was lovely, and the team was welcoming. They began by running through the school's vision and values, all of which were perfectly aligned with mine – amazing! After that we took a quick break, during which the school kitchen team served breakfast for us all. How brilliant! This isn't as scary as I had worried it might be, I thought.

But my confidence did not last long.

What followed was a series of presentations, meetings, and discussions. After each I seemed to know less than I did at the beginning of the day. The conversations were littered with acronyms and initialisms: INSET, EAL, EYFS, PP, SEND, EHCPs, SIMS, GLD, CAMHS, LAC, TAF. My notebook was quickly becoming filled with words I needed to google that evening. Lots of names were being used, but I didn't know who any of these people were. Throughout that day people kept talking about a woman called Diane-Elaine, who I gathered was responsible for safeguarding. I looked around the room, trying to pinpoint which person they were talking about. It would take me three months of working in that school to learn that people were actually saying 'Di and Elaine', two completely separate people. How embarrassing.

I left the hall that day feeling overwhelmed. The language being used in that hall wasn't a language that I understood, and it left me feeling confused, nervous, and at times excluded. I couldn't be part of the conversations that day fully because language was a barrier. In education, we use acronyms, initialisms, and technical vocabulary all of the time. This only works in our schools because that language is understood by everybody: it is a common language.

That is precisely the argument of this chapter: we must develop a common inclusive language so that everybody feels safe, feels seen, feels supported, and is included in the conversations that happen in our educational spaces.

As we explored in Chapter 3, we are all on a journey of learning and unlearning. Any of us working in education will know that mistakes are a part of any journey of learning, and we will all make mistakes as we strive for a common inclusive language. This is as true for me as it is for you.

In our episode with B Guerriero (S1, E5), I made a mistake. I used language that wasn't inclusive and didn't make B feel seen and supported. This exchange (described below) is a good example of how non-inclusive language can hurt a person, how this can be respectfully challenged, and how to apologise when mistakes are made.

B is non-binary, as they defined for us in Chapter 3. During our interview we were having a fascinating conversation about where people's anger towards gender-diverse people comes from. I was suggesting that anger is sometimes rooted in their own shame, or in a resentment towards seeing a level of freedom and expression that people were not granted themselves. While making my point, in one sentence I used the word 'choice'.

After I finished speaking, B picked up on the word 'choice'. They repeated back to me what I had said, and then they explained how that word made them feel. They explained that in using the word choice, I had suggested their identity was something they were choosing, or something that they could have chosen to change. Their challenge was educational, and it was empathetic. They assumed my positive intent but were clear about how my language had hurt them. B explained to us, 'people's identities are important, and so is mine. Being myself is not a phase, a choice, a preference, or a decision – it is just who I am'. They made the point that we would never describe heterosexual or cisgendered people as 'making a choice', and they were right.

I listened to what B said, and I reflected on the language I used. When they had finished speaking, I told them that I was sorry. I thanked them for correcting me, and for explaining how my words had impacted them. I acknowledged that there was work to do to improve my understanding, and I committed to doing that work. B responded, 'I am so glad that we are comfortable in correcting each other', and our conversation continued.

This interaction is a great example of the power of getting empathetic, educational conversations right when challenging language. It is important for us to discuss how we challenge language in a way that is productive, but these challenges are made easier if we can first establish a common goal, and a common inclusive language.

I believe it is essential to establish a common goal for the holistic Diversity, Equity, and Inclusion (DEI) work in any school. A common goal gets every person on the same page, and it gives you a safety net to fall back on if things become challenging.

In the Introduction to this book, we suggested a common goal that we hope we all share: we want every person in our school communities to be free to be themselves, to feel seen, to feel safe, to feel supported, and to feel like they belong. This is an example of a common goal you may establish in your school community.

With a common goal in place, you can take this further by consciously co-constructing a common inclusive language in your school. In Chapter 2 we introduced you to the brilliant leader and ally Kyrstie Stubbs (S1, E8). In our conversation with Kyrstie, she tells us how important developing a common inclusive language was for her school's journey towards greater LGBT+ inclusion. Kyrstie explains there is a lot of language around LGBT+ identities, and this needed to be explored with her school team. They made time to get together and look at these terms, ensuring everybody understood them, and was comfortable with their meaning. Kyrstie then facilitated a conversation about which of these words should be introduced at different age groups in the school. Together, her team co-constructed a progression of inclusive language, so everybody was clear what words were introduced when. Kyrstie explains this isn't necessarily about what is 'appropriate' at different ages, but rather about what age a child, or young person, can comprehend a word like transgender.

As well as developing use of inclusive language in school, Kyrstie tells us it is important to ensure all staff know how to challenge inappropriate non-inclusive language and do so consistently every time they hear it. But, like B, she takes an empathetic and educational approach to these challenges.

It reminds me of a time when I was teaching Year 6, and a child told me the word 'gay' meant 'when a person was pathetic, or not very good at something'. I'm sure we've all heard 'that's so gay' used with that definition. But the child wasn't being unkind. He was using a word in a way that his community had taught him was correct, and in a way which until that day nobody had taught him any better. While there is a place for more serious responses to deliberate hate language being used in schools, empathetic educational conversations should always be our first response.

In Chapter 3 we met Eilidh Vizard (S1, E11), who introduces words like heteronormativity to class discussion, breaking down what the word means and unpicking it as a group. Our conversation with Eilidh also explored how we productively challenge language in school that falls short of our common goal for holistic inclusion. Eilidh tells us how gendered language is so embedded in our schools. She talks to us about the importance of discussing inclusive language with colleagues and challenging any language that might not be inclusive. Eilidh recognises that challenging other people's language can be difficult, or uncomfortable – she tells us that some people can be defensive in response. It is important to find a balance of calling language out (being educational) while remaining respectful (being empathetic).

Again, this is where that common goal is powerful. You can say to a colleague or student:

'We have all agreed that we want our school to be a place where every person is free to be themselves, feel seen, feel safe, feel supported, and feel like they belong. When you use a phrase like "boys and girls", this might not be inclusive for all people, and might make some people feel like they don't belong. Instead, we could use a word like "team".'

It isn't personal, and it isn't critical, it is just acknowledging that a person's language has fallen short of the common goal you have established and suggesting a way to do better together.

Another way to introduce new language, or challenge the misuse of known language, is by using a Frayer Model. David Lowbridge-Ellis (S2, E11) tells us how these work, and how he has seen them impact his school. The Frayer Model, David explains, helps us to use all of the channels in our brain to explore vocabulary. The model, which you can google, is a simple table, with the word you want to explore in the centre. Around the word are four boxes: a box for a definition or explanation; a box for characteristics of this word; a box for examples of it being used; and a box for non-examples showing how it could be misused. In our conversation, David talks us through how he has used this model to unpick the misuse of gay in his school community. By showing what this word does mean with real examples, and what it doesn't mean by pointing out their misuse of it, David was able to effectively challenge the use of that language in his school. Imagine for a moment how this model could be used to explore heteronormativity in your school, or gender. Introducing Frayer Models can be a time commitment, but David argues it is worth it to purposefully construct a common understanding of inclusive language.

I want to share a final story with you that isn't from our podcast. I was recently discussing the concept of a common inclusive language while leading a staff meeting for a school team. During the meeting, one of the teachers told us about a conversation between her and a young trans person from their school. The teacher had asked the young person about the language they use to identify with. The young person had told their teacher that when people use the right language, when they are inclusive, they feel safe, and they feel seen. But when people didn't use the right language around them, then instead they felt invisible.

Invisible.

Surely none of us want that? By consciously using the right language for this young person an educator could instead make them feel safe and seen. This language might include pronouns. I was a primary school teacher for a long time, and pronouns are part of the Primary writing curriculum, often taught in Year 1. The difficulty is, we are often taught to assume a person's pronouns, and indeed assume their gender identity, just from looking at them. Whilst these predictions might often be right, in some cases they won't be, and a person may be left feeling invisible. So rather than making assumptions, we might ask a person what pronouns they use, or better still introduce ourselves using the pronouns we use to give them the opportunity to do the same. You'll notice Adam and I did just that in the introduction to this book. This simple practice, which takes nothing away from you, can give so much to a trans or gender diverse person. It can help them to feel safe and seen, rather than feeling invisible. We don't want any person to feel invisible in our schools. Co-creating a common inclusion goal, and a common inclusive language in your school, allows space for everybody to feel like they belong. As Kyrstie found in the schools she leads, it is one of the first steps towards reimagining your educational space as more inclusive.

IN ACTION

Let's look at that common goal one more time:

Every person in our school community should be free to be themselves, to feel safe, to feel seen, and to feel like they belong.

How could you adapt this to create a common inclusion goal for your setting?

Reflect on the vocabulary introduced so far throughout this book.

What new vocabulary might need to be introduced and understood by your team? How could you co-create an inclusive common language with your team?

Spend some time reflecting on the language used in your educational space.

What language do you need to challenge, and how can you best do this?

PODCAST EPISODES REFERENCED IN THIS CHAPTER

- Season 1, Episode 5 – B Guerriero

B (they/them) is a primary school teacher, LGBT+ youth worker, and a trustee of the UK Literacy Association. They join us to share their experience as a non-binary immigrant navigating a career in education.

- Season 1, Episode 8 – Kyrstie Stubbs

Kyrstie (she/her) is an inspirational former headteacher, now Deputy CEO, and an LGBT+ ally. She joins us to share how her leadership approaches diversity, equity, and inclusion in a holistic, and meaningful way.

- Season 1, Episode 11 – Eilidh Vizard

Eilidh (she/her) is a secondary school science teacher. She joins us to discuss inclusive language, and representation for LGBT+ people, and women in STEM.

- Season 2, Episode 11 – David Lowbridge-Ellis

David (he/they) is a headteacher, writer and trainer. He joins us to share brilliant tips on how to make educational spaces more inclusive, and how to be an effective and authentic leader.

REFERENCES

Barker, M. (2016). *Queer: A Graphic History.* Icon Books.

Ferfolja, T. (2007). Schooling cultures: Institutionalizing heteronormativity and heterosexism. *International Journal of Inclusive Education, 11* (2), pp. 147–162. https://doi.org/10.1080/13603110500296596

Government Equalities Office (2010). Equality Act 2010: guidance. www.gov.uk/guidance/equality-act-2010-guidance

Nadal, K.L., Whitman, C.N., Davis, L.S., et al. (2016). Microaggressions toward lesbian, gay, bisexual, transgender, queer, and genderqueer people: A review of the literature. *The Journal of Sex Research, 53* (4–5), pp. 488–508.

Pellegrini, A. (1992). S(h)ifting the terms of hetero/sexism: Gender, power, homophobias. In W. Blumenfeld (Ed.), *Homophobia: How we all Pay the Price*. Beacon Press, pp. 39–56.

Rich, A. (1994). *Blood, Bread, and Poetry: Selected prose 1979–1985.* WW Norton & Company.

Sue, D.W., Bucceri, J., Lin, A.I., Nadal, K.L., & Torino, G.C. (2007) Racial microaggressions and the Asian American experience. *Cultural Diversity and Ethnic Minority Psychology, 13*(1), pp. 72–81.

5

CURRICULUM, REPRESENTATION, AND VISIBILITY

'I see it as my moral duty to educate children for the world in which they live.'

Kyrstie Stubbs

IN THEORY

In many ways, curriculum is the Ant to language's Dec; the Obama to its Michelle; the Barry to its Paul (I may have wandered into the niche here…), but suffice to say, the two go hand-in-hand. Once teachers are equipped with the right language, they can really unleash the power of the curriculum to reveal the rich and diverse LGBT+ history that has been hidden there all along. Can you imagine the impact it would have had if your English teacher had presented a nuanced discussion about William Shakespeare's sexuality based upon his sonnets, or if your geography teacher had examined the multiple understandings of gender in societies around the world? Small changes like this not only make our curriculums more interesting, but much more importantly, it makes them inclusive.

So, what is a curriculum? We could think of it as the diet that we feed to our students. A menu of carefully curated topics, ideas, concepts, and skills that our young people require to be well-rounded and successful citizens. The question is, who is deciding what goes on the menu? Debates about what should and shouldn't be included within the curriculum will exist for as long as education does – and quite right, too. Curriculums need to be regularly evaluated and adapted to ensure our young people are being prepared for a rapidly changing future. Schools have the impossible task of trying to educate students for jobs that don't even exist yet. While it is difficult to predict what education our young people may need for their future careers, there is one set of skills we can guarantee that people will always need: kindness and empathy.

'You can't be what you can't see' is a phrase that's often used in education; a statement so simultaneously simple yet profound, that I feel it should be written in huge letters on every staff room wall in the country. As part of my job, I visit a lot of schools and, when walking the corridors, I often think of this axiom. I try to put myself in the shoes of the young people that attend there. I wonder if they can see a place for themselves in the school, and as importantly, a place for themselves in the world. Growing up during Section 28, I was denied an inclusive education and so am acutely aware of the importance of being able to see yourself in the curriculum. Schools are wonderful and transformative places, with the power to truly improve children's lives. This is a privilege, but also a responsibility, and not one we should take lightly. Schools should be places where students witness the full spectrum of human experience, where they see and read about people that look just like them, and develop empathy and understanding about those who don't.

> Books are sometimes windows, offering views of worlds that may be real or imagined, familiar or strange. These windows are also sliding glass doors, and readers have only to walk through in imagination to become part of whatever world has been created or recreated by the author. When lighting conditions are just right, however, a window can also be a mirror. Literature transforms human experience and reflects it back to us, and in that reflection we can see our own lives and experiences as part of a larger human experience. Reading, then, becomes a means of self-affirmation, and readers often seek their mirrors in books.
>
> (Bishop 1990)

As Bishop describes, more beautifully than I ever could, the literature we use, and as an extension, the curriculums we teach, should act as windows and mirrors. The mirrors should reflect students and their experiences, so they feel seen, validated, and able to imagine a future for themselves. The curriculum should also serve as windows that students can look through to see lives, experiences, and perspectives different to their own. By including LGBT+ content within the curriculum, we are making our LGBT+ students (and staff) feel seen and included. We are also developing empathy and kindness in all our students. I love the aphorism, 'there is a cure for ignorance: education', as it reminds us of the wider responsibility we have to our students; to help them become compassionate, empathetic, and open-minded citizens. While this is an important and empowering mission statement, how to go about it can often feel like a separate challenge. As classroom teachers, the curriculum can sometimes feel like a monolith; something unchangeable that we must deliver without question. However, we don't need to tear up and redesign the curriculum to ensure it is LGBT+ inclusive. As Karan brilliantly says in the podcast, the curriculum is already queer, it just needs to be revealed!

Depending on your seniority in school, you may be questioning how much impact over the curriculum you are able to have. The influence that school leaders can have will be explored in Chapter 8, but we argue that classroom teachers are the ones with the opportunity to make the biggest impact. In reading this book, you have already recognised there is a need for greater LGBT+ inclusivity in the classroom and that you wish to make positive change. The good news is, making your teaching inclusive of LGBT+ lives is actually quite easy. Once you begin seeing the simple ways that lessons can become LGBT+ inclusive, it quickly becomes second nature to include within your planning. The even better news is that a lot of this work has already been done for you! There are a huge amount of excellent, free resources from organisations such as Schools Out, Educate and Celebrate, Just Like Us, and Stonewall available for you to use. You can google each of these organisations to browse their terrific resources, but two that are worthy of mention here are Stonewall's *Creating an LGBTQ+ Inclusive Primary Curriculum* (2022) and *Creating an LGBTQ+ Inclusive Secondary Curriculum* (2018). These two resources contain ideas, lesson plans and schemes of work for almost every subject. They show the big and small ways in which LGBT+ lives can be usualised within the curriculum, from a full maths lesson looking at code breaking and Alan Turing, to simply changing the wording of a question, for example, 'Mark's dads increase his pocket money by 10%. If Mark had £2 before the increase, how much pocket money does he have now?'. These are minor changes that can have enormous and lasting impact.

You may have noticed I used the word usualise in the previous paragraph, which Jo has also used throughout the book. This is a term coined for the Schools Out for the Classroom model by the formidable Professor Emeritus, Sue Sanders (S2, E1). Sue gave an empowering TED talk in 2021 entitled 'visibilising and usualising the LGBTQ+ community', in which she examines how and why LGBT+ lives have historically been hidden within the curriculum.

Queer history had been deliberately hidden. It was very deliberately hidden.

(Sanders 2021)

Sue argues that it's vital we include LGBT+ visibility in the curriculum and demonstrates how we can most effectively do this through the process of usualising. Sue explains that 'normal' is a pejorative term and leads to the concept of 'abnormal'. She argues if we usualise, then 'we get rid of the gay lesson, [we get rid of] the black lesson, and what we do is embed all the marginalised groups into every lesson... we become usual, every day, ordinary'. Sue further explains that there needs to be diverse and intersectional representations of LGBT+ people, as visibility often defaults to that of white, able-bodied, gay men. While it can be simple to bring LGBT+ visibility into our curriculum, we must be conscious that we are presenting a broad and balanced view of the LGBT+ community, particularly for trans identities. Greytak, Kosciw and Boesen (2013) argue that when we are discussing LGBT+ inclusive education, it is important that we give equal or greater emphasis to the lives and experiences of trans people, recognising the distinct differences and challenges they may experience compared to their cis peers.

With a little bit of research and planning, we can transform our lessons to usualise a broad range of LGBT+ identities, creating the mirrors our LGBT+ students desperately need, and the windows to kindness and empathy that enrich the lives of our cisgender and heterosexual students. However, curriculum isn't the only way we can make visible. Sexuality and gender are often invisible in ways that other protected characteristics aren't. It is for this reason that we need to metaphorically, and literally, fly the rainbow flag.

As an adult, whenever I see a rainbow pride flag, it is a subtle but powerful signifier that I am in a safe place or talking to an understanding person. Seeing a shop with a pride sticker in the window or speaking to a colleague with a pin badge on their lanyard is something that can mean a lot. This small gesture may be something that most people don't notice, but to me, it communicates that I am in a safe space or with a person that has an understanding and empathy of what it is to be LGBT+. I'm always reassured to see these symbols in environments that sometimes feel quite heteronormative or even hostile, such as a car garage or gym. Sadly, but perhaps not surprisingly, a lot of the existing research shows that LGBT+ teachers often find the school staff room a heteronormative or uncomfortable space.

If these symbols can mean this much to me as an adult, imagine how much they can mean for the young people in our schools who are still exploring their identities. Wearing a pin badge or displaying a flag in your classroom is a small but powerful way of communicating to students that they are in a safe place. It's also a brilliant way of puncturing the inherent heteronormativity and cisnormativity of schools. I have had some of the best and most important conversations in my classroom where students have asked why I wear a rainbow lanyard or share my pronouns.

So far, we've briefly thought about how we can adapt our curriculum to usualise LGBT+ lives, and how we can create visibility through symbols such as lanyards, badges, and posters. The final powerful thing we can do is provide our students with a diverse range of representation and role models. As a business teacher, I am uncomfortably aware of the lack of diversity that sits within the A Level curriculum. Curriculums are supposed to present our students with the 'best of what has been thought and said'. Almost every theorist we learn about in business is male, pale, and stale; or to use Scotty Cartwright's (S1, E15) acronym, SWORD (straight, white, old, rich, and dead). Are we really teaching our students that the best of what has been thought and said comes exclusively from straight white men? It feels negligent to present my students with a two-year course that contains zero female representation. This is also true for LGBT+ representation and it is why I go out of my way to ensure I have displays spotlighting diverse LGBT+ entrepreneurs and CEOs like Tim Cook, Moriaki Kida and Beth Ford. Have a think about the role models and representation that exist within your curriculum and classroom – can students see diverse role models and representation, including LGBT+ people?

There are many subjects in which LGBT+ representation and role models remain scant. We have seen the huge push that has taken place in recent years to get women into STEM subjects, and the same level of effort is required to get LGBT+ students into underrepresented subjects. Sport remains an area that while improving, can be isolating for LGBT+ people, especially in secondary school where students are exploring their sexual and gender identities. I ran a CPD session for the Heads of Sport in our Trust recently and talked about some of the ideas from this chapter. The staff went on to make some small but impactful changes, including gender-neutral changing room options, displays of LGBT+ athletes, rainbow shoelaces, and mixed gender activities. A few months later, the Director of Sport came to tell me that a student who was trans and hadn't taken part in sport for three years was now attending regularly and had joined the rugby team. They hadn't realised how distressing sport can be for LGBT+ people, and similarly couldn't believe the huge impact these small changes could have.

Next time you're in school, have a walk around the building. Put yourself in the shoes of a student questioning their gender or sexual identity and think about the spaces in which you can and can't see representations of yourself. Think about the classrooms you would feel safe in and the staff that you would feel comfortable talking to – what do these things have in common? Teaching is an incredibly busy and stressful job and making your classroom LGBT+ inclusive may feel like a difficult and time-consuming task. Hopefully, this chapter highlights some of the small changes we can all make that go a long way to ensure our LGBT+ students feel safe, seen and celebrated.

IN PRACTICE

At the time of publishing, Pride & Progress has been running for two years. During that time, we've completed two podcast seasons and just started a third, releasing over 30 episodes including conversations with over 40 brilliant guests, facilitated book clubs, built support networks, delivered professional development training, and spent countless hours talking to educators about LGBT+ inclusive education.

This isn't me shamelessly bragging. Well, maybe it is – but it is shameless bragging with a point. My point being that throughout all the work we have done with Pride & Progress, I can't think of a single conversation we have had about inclusive education which hasn't spoken about curriculum, representation, and visibility. These three elements, combined with the common inclusive language discussed in the previous chapter, are the four pillars of inclusive education.

With these four pillars firmly in place, educators can build an LGBT+ inclusive educational space. With any or all of them not firm as a foundation, the inclusive space you're attempting to build may fall.

We have already explored the damage that can be done when an LGBT+ person grows up without representation, or visible, relatable role models. Remember how Helen (S2, E2) described being cheated out of a sound start in life, and being limited in how she imagined her life could play out? We hear similar points echoed in many of our conversations where people grew up without the four pillars in place holding up inclusion.

During our conversation with Ian Eagleton and James Mayhew (S1, E10) we discuss what representation looked like for them as students, and how this experience motivates the work they do now. James was born at a time when being gay was illegal; he explains what it was like to grow up with no books, no helplines, no role models, and no internet. Like many of us, James first heard words he would later identify with used as insults in hateful bullying. This environment caused James to convince himself that being gay was not an option for him, and that he could convince himself he wasn't. James went on to marry a woman and have a child – a great source of joy in his life, which he of course doesn't regret. But he talks candidly about how LGBT+ visibility during his education could have saved a lot of people a great deal of heartache later in life.

Ian was born later than James, starting school in the early 1990s. He tells us that throughout all his education he saw no LGBT+ representation. The lack of education meant that he experienced regular violent and verbal bullying throughout school. He couldn't tell anybody about it, because to do so would mean coming out publicly. He couldn't tell teachers, his friends, or his family about the violence he was experiencing. Instead, Ian started to escape by writing stories featuring himself – he created worlds where he could belong, have adventure, and feel joy.

Now, both James and Ian are thriving – but it has taken work to get to that point. James lives with his husband and their dog and is a wonderfully talented artist and illustrator. Ian lives with his husband and child and is the author of several brilliant and LGBT+ inclusive books. One of which, *Nen and the Lonely Fisherman*, was illustrated by James, and won the inaugural Children's & YA Polari Prize. They joined us on the podcast to discuss working together on this book. They both suggest how much their lives would have been changed if there was LGBT+ representation in the books they read as students in school. They argue that LGBT+ representation and visibility is as important for heterosexual, cisgender young people as it is for those who identify within the LGBT+ community. Books like Ian and James' are important in offering hope and support to LGBT+ young people, but they also offer the opportunity for all young people to see differences, to usualise diversity, and to build empathy with people who are not like them. Imagine how those bullies might have behaved differently if they had heard LGBT+ people spoken about positively throughout school? James says these books are about giving all people a wider spectrum of things to hope about, dream about, and wish for. While Ian describes them as a model of hope, for all children.

Diversifying your school library and looking closely at the books studied in your school can have a big impact. We've already discussed the power of hearing lived experiences, and fictional stories can be equally powerful. We only have to look at the impact of *Heartstopper* to see the potential power of inclusive stories.

Heartstopper is a British coming-of-age story of romance based on the graphic novels of the same name by the brilliant Alice Oseman. The story follows a group of young LGBT+ people as they navigate falling in love. It quickly became one of Netflix's most critically acclaimed shows and was within the top 10 watched shows in over 60 different countries.

We had a *Heartstopper* special episode (S2, E8), where we were joined by George White, Karan Bhumbla, Allison Zionts, and Aisling Walters to discuss the impact of the story. Aisling Walters is an English PGCE Senior Lecturer, a fan of *Heartstopper*, and a brilliant ally to the LGBT+ community. On the panel she tells us how stories like *Heartstopper* 'offer young people a space to find themselves'. Aisling praises the author Alice Oseman for making all of these stories freely available to read on her website. In doing so, Alice has created a safe space for young people to find themselves. We also spoke with one of the actors from the show, Fisayo Akinade (S2, E9). Through both conversations we hear how important the LGBT+ representation this story offers has been for young people in schools. We hear directly from teachers who have seen real change in their schools as a result of engagement with this story.

As I listened back to those two conversations, it was amazing to hear the power of just one story. Stories matter, and while diversifying the books in your schools is a small action, it can have a huge impact on representation and visibility in your setting.

Actually, many of the most effective ways to improve LGBT+ representation in schools are small. Kyrstie Stubbs (S1, E8) shares with us lots of quick wins for visibility: displaying LGBT+ people in your corridor displays; having rainbow flags, or rainbow lanyards for staff; in her Early Years spaces, Kyrstie ensures her toys and dolls are diverse; and the staff in her school are conscious of displaying diversity and difference in their classroom presentations.

A lot of the educators we speak to also talk about the power of using assemblies to introduce visible LGBT+ role models. Helen (S2, E2) has created a full year assembly plan in her school which introduced a wide variety of diverse role models and intersectional identities to the young people in her school. Her assemblies have had great feedback from students, staff, and families.

While assemblies can be powerful, representation doesn't need to be timetabled. Allison (S1, E3) takes opportunities with her form group to celebrate positive LGBT+ news stories or highlight significant LGBT+ people who are achieving great things. These conversations can take 30 seconds, but it shows young people that LGBT+ people not only exist but can thrive. Allison tells us how important it is to ensure our representation is hopeful, and not always focusing on the discrimination that LGBT+ people face.

These small changes can have a big impact. By introducing LGBT+ representation and visibility, we offer an alternative blueprint. We give young LGBT+ people the chance to see that they can belong, and we give all young people the opportunity to build empathy and usualise acceptance and respect for diversity. Of course, there is a bigger conversation to be had about curriculum more broadly.

As well as the small actions to improve visibility, Kyrstie's (S1, E8) school also has an extended curriculum that sits alongside the National Curriculum and teaches students in her school about DEI. Bigger curriculum work like this is time consuming and requires careful planning, but as Kyrstie explains, it is our moral duty to educate children for the world in which they live.

David Lowbridge-Ellis (S2, E11) is another excellent leader who has developed a more inclusive curriculum in his school. David recognises that teachers are time-poor, and often find themselves wrestling with what to prioritise. He explains that if we want people to change, and to make LGBT+ inclusion a priority, then we must make that change easy for them. Building LGBT+ representation into our curriculum ensures that visibility and makes it easier for teachers to represent LGBT+ people.

A task that might take more time is looking at your school year and ensuring you mark key dates like Transgender Awareness Day, or Pride Month. There are great resources to support you in this work. Sue Sanders (S2, E1) co-founded LGBT+ History Month, which is now marked by many schools. In our conversation with Sue, we were also joined by Lynne Nicholls who is the Chair of Trustees for Schools Out. Lynne talks us through the wonderful resources available to support LGBT+ History Month, which you can find easily through their website. Similarly, Schools Diversity Week is a great opportunity to build inclusion into your curriculum offer. Dominic Arnall (S1, E4), the former CEO of Just Like Us, tells us the week is not about putting LGBT+ people into the curriculum, but instead about no longer taking them out. 'LGBT+ people are part of society, they always have been, so let's make sure they are threaded through the curriculum', he explains.

Of course, it is also possible for LGBT+ educators themselves to become positive representatives and visible role models within their settings. Many of the educators we have introduced you to in this book have done that, and the impact in every case is astounding. In our conversation with George (S1, E2) we talk about how an out teacher can attach a real person to a label that many young people will have preconceived ideas about: it can humanise an identity. However, an LGBT+ person should never feel pressure to come out. Being open about your identity as an LGBT+ educator should always be the choice of the individual, and they should only do so if they feel safe and comfortable in sharing that part of themselves. Karan (S1, E6) warns that no one should be a role model at the expense of their own well-being and is clear that being visible is secondary to being safe.

As we've heard, there is brilliant work being done around curriculum and LGBT+ representation in schools. However, currently this is a postcode lottery where there is great work being done, in the schools where work is being done. In other areas, LGBT+ representation is still limited. If representation is limited, then the lives we allow young LGBT+ people to imagine for themselves are limited, too. It is like asking them to build a jigsaw without allowing them to see the box which has the picture on it. It is an unnecessary challenge; it makes it harder for them to build an understanding of who they are. We hope that reading this chapter has encouraged you to ensure your education space is one where good work is being done: a space where LGBT+ people are represented and visible; and a space where we allow young people to imagine a wide variety of possible lives for themselves.

This book began by setting out some of the larger barriers we face when striving for LGBT+ inclusive education, where all people can be themselves, feel safe, feel seen, and feel like they belong. The history of non-inclusive education is still rooted in our schools, and we see that played out through hetero/cisnormative environments. These last two chapters have set out the pillars that we need to ensure are firmly in place to begin reimagining our educational spaces and building them to be more LGBT+ inclusive.

As you now know, we end each chapter with an opportunity to reflect and move this discussion into action within your own setting. Please, take your time with this next reflection opportunity. In discussing language, curriculum, visibility, and representation we have shared a lot of information and best practice. Take the time to think about what this means for you and your setting.

When you've had time to reflect, we'll be moving on to the second half of this book. Having identified the barriers, and discussed the most important starting points to overcome those barriers, we will now turn to explore several other themes which will be important to consider: community and connection; intersectionality; leadership; personal and professional identity; and finally allyship and advocacy.

IN ACTION

Reflect on what is visible in your school – if possible, take a walk around.

Who is clearly and visibly represented in your school space?

Reflect on the opportunities for macro representation and visibility.

What small changes could you make to your daily curriculum to usualise LGBTQ+ identities within your school?

Now, and this point might take a little longer, think more deeply about your curriculum on a macro level.

How does your curriculum represent the diversity of society, and where are the gaps that need filling?

PODCAST EPISODES REFERENCED IN THIS CHAPTER

- Season 1, Episode 10 – Ian Eagleton & James Mayhew

Ian (he/him) was a primary school teacher for 13 years, and is now an author, and creator of The Reading Realm. James (he/him) is an artist and children's book illustrator. They join us to share their experience working on the beautifully inclusive fairytale: *Nen and The Lonely Fisherman*.

- Season 2, Episode 8 – *Heartstopper* Special

In this episode the hosts of Pride & Progress assemble some special friends of the show to discuss the Netflix series *Heartstopper*, and the impact this story is having in schools.

- Season 2, Episode 9 – Fisayo Akinade

Fisayo (he/him) is a brilliant actor of both screen and stage, and plays Mr Ajayi in the Netflix show *Heartstopper*. He joins us to discuss his career in acting, and his role in *Heartstopper* portraying an LGBT+ educator.

- Season 1, Episode 8 – Kyrstie Stubbs

Kyrstie (she/her) is an inspirational former headteacher, now Deputy CEO, and an LGBT+ ally. She joins us to share how her leadership approaches diversity, equity, and inclusion in a holistic, and meaningful way.

- Season 2, Episode 2 – Helen Richardson

Helen Richardson (she/her) is a deputy headteacher and led the diversity network for her school's Trust. Helen joins us to share her experience growing up during Section 28, and now working as an out, lesbian educator.

- Season 1, Episode 3 – Allison Zionts

Allison (she/her) is a secondary school teacher and PhD researcher exploring LGBTQ+ safe spaces. She joins us to discuss her research, and share her experience as a bisexual, Jewish woman.

- Season 2, Episode 11 – David Lowbridge-Ellis

David (he/they) is a headteacher, writer and trainer. He joins us to share brilliant tips on how to make educational spaces more inclusive, and how to be an effective and authentic leader.

- Season 2, Episode 1 – Professor Emeritus Sue Sanders & Lynne Nicholls

Sue (she/her) is an inspirational educator and the co-founder of LGBT+ History Month. Lynne (she/her) is the Chair of Trustees for charity Schools Out. They join us to discuss the history of LGBT+ inclusive education, LGBT+ History Month, and the work of Schools Out.

- Season 1, Episode 4 – Dominic Arnall

Dominic (he/him) was the CEO of LGBT+ young people's charity 'Just Like Us' at the time we spoke. He joins us to discuss the great work that Just Like Us does to support LGBT+ young people and schools.

- Season 1, Episode 2 – George White

George (he/him) is a teacher of Religious Education, inclusion leader, and LGBTQ+ inclusion consultant. He joins us to share his experience as a trans man now teaching in the same Catholic school he attended as a student.

- Season 1, Episode 6 – Karan Bhumbla

Karan (he/him) is a secondary school science teacher. He joins us to share his experience as a gay, Indian science teacher working to be a positive representation for all facets of his identity.

REFERENCES

Bishop, R. S. (1990). Windows and mirrors: Children's books and parallel cultures. Paper presented at the California State University Reading Conference: 14th Annual Conference Proceedings, 3–12.

Greytak, E.A., Kosciw, J.G., & Boesen, M.J. (2013). Putting the 'T' in 'resource': The benefits of LGBT-related school resources for transgender youth. *Journal of LGBT Youth, 10* (1–2), pp. 45–63.

Sanders, S. (2021). 'Visibilising and Usualising' the LGBTQ+ Community. www.ted.com/talks/sue_sanders_visibilising_and_usualising_the_lgbtq_community

Stonewall (2018). *Creating an LGBTQ+ inclusive secondary curriculum.* www.stonewall.org.uk/system/files/z_inclusive_secondary_curriculum_guide_-_august_2022.pdf

Stonewall (2022). *Creating an LGBTQ+ inclusive primary curriculum.* www.stonewall.org.uk/system/files/stw_pearson_creating_an_inclusive_primary_curriculum_2022_1_-_march.pdf

6

COMMUNITY AND CONNECTION

> *'We can all do so much more if we feel supported, and if we feel there is a network of people there to help us.'*
>
> *Nick Kitchener-Bentley*

IN THEORY

Given the inherent cis/heteronormativity of schools, LGBT+ people can often feel untethered or disconnected in educational spaces. I remember starting my career and thinking I must be the only LGBT+ teacher in the world. There was no visibility or discussion of LGBT+ educators in my training or early years, leaving me to think that the anxieties I had about being a gay teacher weren't real or valid. Even now, if you look at the Core Content Framework that underpins teacher training, there is no mention or consideration that teachers from minority groups may experience different challenges in the classroom and therefore require additional support. I worked for a headteacher once who, after I told him I was gay, said 'I don't care if you're gay or you're straight, I treat all people the same.' While he was very proud of his somewhat myopic worldview, all it served to do was ignore and diminish the challenges I and other LGBT+ people in the school experienced. If equality is treating everyone the same, then this headteacher was nailing it; however, LGBT+ staff and students don't need equality, they need equity. We need to acknowledge that LGBT+ people may experience additional challenges compared to their cis and straight peers and therefore require extra support to make them feel part of a school community. Meyer's (2003) Minority Stress Theory is a good way of conceptualising what these challenges may look like.

> One elaboration of social stress theory may be referred to as minority stress to distinguish the excess stress to which individuals from stigmatised social categories are exposed as a result of their social, often a minority, position.
>
> (Meyer 2003)

Meyer's Minority Stress Theory identifies that all people experience general stressors – the stresses that daily life can cause, especially when in a school. Minority stress refers to the additional stressors that LGBT+ people may experience. Meyer describes two types of stressors: distal and proximal. Distal stressors refer to experiences such as homophobic or transphobic discrimination or abuse; proximal stressors refer to the internal impact these events may have caused, such as expectations of rejection, or experiences of isolation or anxiety. You would struggle to find an LGBT+ person who hasn't experienced distal stress in their life, and it is this that schools need to be aware of. If LGBT+ people have experienced or even witnessed discrimination before, they internalise this, and the fear of it potentially happening to them can be just as distressing as it actually happening. In my doctoral research, a lot of my participants experienced this fear-of-something-happening stress in panoptic or unregulated spaces, e.g., when out on duty or in the dining hall, and consequently, felt discomfort when navigating these types of space within school.

Think about some of the things an LGBT+ person might be nervous about in a school setting. What if students use slurs towards me? Do I share my gender or sexuality on the application form? What if my gender/sexual identity isn't recognised? What title or pronouns do I use? Can I come out? To whom? Is there a conflict with religion? What uniform do I wear? Which facilities do I use? How do I navigate social situations? How do I answer personal questions? This fear of discrimination and constant two-steps-ahead assessment of risk can be truly exhausting for LGBT+ people. Straight and cis people have access to frictionless movement around schools, meaning they don't need to continuously anticipate and negotiate their surroundings; we could describe this as a form of privilege. Reflecting back on my earlier example – why did it grate so much when the headteacher told me he treats everybody the same? Because his privilege didn't allow him to recognise that people with minority identities may have a more challenging experience of school compared to their peers and, therefore, may need additional care and support.

This is where community and connection come in. If you are an LGBT+ person, I imagine you nodded along while reading the last couple of paragraphs as you have a tacit understanding of the things I have described. This is why spaces for LGBT+ people are so important; they provide a place for people with a shared understanding and lived experience to come together and feel safe. In these spaces, stressors are removed, experiences are understood, and defences are lowered, all allowing LGBT+ people to be their authentic selves. There's a wonderful moment in the film *Love Simon* where Simon comes out to his mum, and after she gives a masterclass in all the right things to say (only rivalled by Olivia Colman in *Heartstopper*), she tells him, 'You get to exhale now, Simon'. I feel this is what LGBT+ people get to do in these spaces; they get to experience connection among a community of people that 'get it'.

What I have described so far has been viewed through the lens of LGBT+ teachers, but if we picture this through the lens of a young person exploring their identity, the importance of community and safer spaces becomes even more significant. Creating spaces where LGBT+ students get to 'breathe' and find their community is one of the most important things a school can do. A well-run LGBT+ club allows students to explore their identities, learn about LGBT+ inclusion, and crucially, create a sense of community. Schools run these types of groups in different ways, but a common key to success is inviting both LGBT+ and non-LGBT+ people. This not only allows people to attend without the need to out themselves, but it also allows non-LGBT+ people to become allies who can develop their empathy and understanding about lives different to their own. Setting up an LGBT+ club may seem daunting, but there is lots of support available, and Just Like Us have a 12-month programme which supports schools in getting started.

Safer spaces for LGBT+ students and staff are crucial and go a long way in reducing some of the stress they may experience. However, the need for safer spaces also highlights the fact that schools often aren't experienced as inclusive by LGBT+ people. Schools need to take a holistic approach to LGBT+ inclusion and, in turn, need to think about what a school community is and who is a part of it. A school community isn't just the teachers and students; it's the teaching assistants, the librarians, the kitchen staff, the cleaners, the governors, the site staff, the parents and carers, as well as so many others. If schools want to create a sense of community, they need to think about all the people that belong to that community. Educate and Celebrate are an excellent organisation who recognise the need for this holistic approach and run training that includes all members of a school so discrimination can be tackled at every level. By ensuring that all members of its community have received quality LGBT+ training, schools can aim to reduce the stressors its LGBT+ populations may experience and increase their sense of belonging and inclusion.

I mentioned parents and carers in the list of people that belong to a school community; however, this is a group of people schools often don't give enough attention to when doing LGBT+ inclusive work. You only need to think about some of the protests that have taken place outside UK schools to understand the moral panic that can take hold when parents are ill-informed about the LGBT+ education taking place. Much of the parental furore making headlines the last few years has been underpinned by outdated and dangerous stereotypes, such as LGBT+ teachers being paedophiles; children becoming sexualised; or that young people are being taught to be LGBT+. While it's tempting to not entertain the views of parents that hold anti-LGBT+ beliefs, we need to take a breath and recognise that at its core, parents just want what is best for their children. When we frame parental backlash as this and begin to unpick the reasons for disquiet, we can see that parents' concerns aren't always as inflammatory as headlines suggest, and that their fears may simply be that their child is being taught something that they don't fully understand themselves. Understanding the reluctance of parents means we can address their concerns in ways that help to individually reassure, while tempering group hysteria. Once parents understand that what their children are being taught is first, age appropriate, and second, designed to ensure that all members of a school feel safe, seen and included, they quickly realise that there is nothing to fear. Andrew Moffat explains one of the most effective ways to do this is to ensure that LGBT+ inclusion sits among a broader programme of inclusivity work, where all members of a school's diverse community are recognised and included as part of the school culture.

While on the topic of parents, we also need to take a brief moment to talk about LGBT+ parents. LGBT+ parented families often have a challenging relationship with school and can struggle to feel part of the community. It's perhaps not surprising when you think that most parents went to school at a time when LGBT+ inclusion was problematic, as described in Chapter 1. Carlile and Paechter (2018) have written a superb book called *LGBTQI Parented Families and Schools*, which explores some of the challenges that LGBT+ parents experience, including simple things such as school forms that only have space for 'mother's name' and 'father's name'; not feeling represented in their child's curriculum; or documentation and school policies that have no reference to LGBT+ parented families. In thinking about the experiences of LGBT+ parents, schools can make small changes that can make these families feel seen and included as part of the school community.

It's been interesting thinking about what community means while writing this chapter. If I think about the schools I've worked in, and the ones where I've thrived, it had nothing to do with the physical building and everything to do with the people and how I was made to feel. Community is about connection and feeling seen, it's about being understood and feeling appreciated, and it's about being a part of something where you can positively contribute. I started this chapter by discussing minority stress and I'm keenly aware that I don't want to contribute to deficit models for LGBT+ people. While it is important to acknowledge the challenges, it is only helpful to do so if solutions are being offered, which hopefully this book does. The raison d'etre of Pride & Progress is sharing positive and hopeful narratives about LGBT+ inclusion in education. We hope the community that we have created through our podcast and this book, that you are now a part of, gives you an insight into the wonderful things that can happen when people find their community. I can confidently say that getting to be a part of this community with Jo and all of you has been one of the best and most rewarding things I've gotten to do in my career. If we can create this sense of community in our classrooms and schools, just think about the ways in which our LGBT+ staff and students could flourish!

IN PRACTICE

In the early summer of 2020, with most of Europe in their own variation of COVID-19 lockdown, we all found ourselves to differing degrees experiencing isolation. Some of us began organising online quizzes with friends, while others decorated their windows with pictures and messages for neighbours to read on their daily walks. Videos of groups of people singing together on their apartment balconies went viral on social media, and waving at a loved one from the bottom of the drive became the highlight of many of our days. During that time, I spent hours writing letters to friends and family. I'd never written letters before but writing them made me feel closer to the people I was forced to be physically distant from.

As lockdowns lifted and restrictions dissolved, many of us emerged with a renewed appreciation of our social freedom. Being forced to distance ourselves physically from the people we love helped us all to realise the importance of community and connection.

Think about the spaces in your lives where you feel that real community and meaningful connection – how special they are! Spaces where you feel togetherness, where our story overlaps with the stories of the people around us, where we become connected, and we all feel less alone.

We all deserve those spaces, and their value cannot be overstated. Let's explore what community and connection looks like in practice for some of our podcast guests.

Adam began this chapter by outlining why community is important for LGBT+ people. In Chapter 3 we learnt that B (S1, E5) was 26 when they first found their community and made connections with people like them. They speak about how transformative that was for them. Helen (S2, E2) had a similarly transformative experience when she started to meet with other LGBT+ educators, and these connections inspired her work.

Some people are lucky to find that community in their workplace. Edel Cronin is an inspirational vice principal and works alongside English teacher and Head of House Aaron Brooks. They are both LGBT+ people and join us to discuss the work they do together in their school (S2, E4). Collectively, they have made huge positive changes to LGBT+ inclusion in their school. In our conversation, they tell us how coming together has empowered them in this work and provided them with a support network.

This kind of connection is powerful, but it isn't available to us all. However, there are fantastic communities available for LGBT+ educators to engage with. #DiverseEd started as a grassroots network founded by Hannah Wilson (S1, E14) and Bennie Kara (S2, E5). Diverse Educators Ltd is now a training company committed to raising the profile of DEI in schools. You can connect with Diverse Educators on social media, or through their website which is a brilliant one-stop-shop for DEI work in schools. Through their directory, you can find other networks that can support LGBT+ educators, including our Pride & Progress network, and LGBTed. Daniel Tomlinson-Gray (S2, E7) is a secondary teacher and the co-founder and director of LGBTed: a network for LGBT+ teachers and leaders. You can connect with their network through their website, or on social media.

Adam and I have found social media a great tool for building LGBT+ educator connections. In our conversation with Nick Kitchener-Bentley (S2, E12) we discuss the pros and cons of these grassroots social media spaces. Nick is a secondary school teacher of Drama and English, and is a wonderfully positive and encouraging voice in education. Through Twitter, Nick connected with Diverse Educators and LGBTed. He's now part of the LGBTed steering group and contributed to the book: *Diverse Educators: A Manifesto*. Nick summarises the power of these groups, 'we can all do so much more if we feel supported, and if we feel there is a network of people there to help us'.

In the same way that community is important for LGBT+ educators, it is equally important for LGBT+ young people. Allison (S1, E3) is the teacher responsible for leading the 'Rainbow Group' in her school. In Allison's experience, it has taken time and energy to build an authentic, safer space for her LGBT+ students and allies, but she tells us how important this space has been. This message is echoed in our conversation with Adam Breslin (S1, E12), who started his own school's Pride group with the support of Stonewall training. Adam emphasises the importance of this space, but also recognises the additional work required to run it on top of other teaching responsibilities. Adam's solution to this challenge was to hand power and ownership over to the students who make up the group. Now, Adam facilitates the space, but it is really the LGBT+ young people who run it. This is a powerful shift from creating the space that adults guess young people may need, to the young LGBT+ people carving their own space in a way that is meaningful for them. They take leadership and mark key events in the calendar, help to develop curriculum, and find ways to challenge discriminatory language around school.

Starting your own pride group can feel daunting, but you don't have to do it alone. Like Adam, you can pull support from charities. Dominic (S1, E4), the former CEO of Just Like Us, shares some great advice for teachers at the beginning of this journey. He tells us that these groups can be one of the most effective things a school can do to embed LGBT+ inclusion. He is also clear that these groups are open to LGBT+ students and allies. This increases the capacity of the safer space, but also prevents anybody from feeling they must out themselves to be part of the group. Like Adam, Dominic also advocates for greater student leadership of these groups.

Student leadership is a common theme in all our conversations about successful LGBT+ groups in school. For Edel and Aaron, it is how their group began. Together, they had been working to celebrate key events in the school calendar and to diversify their curriculum. One day, pupils told them that although this work is important, it wasn't considering the fact they were still experiencing homophobia in school. The pupils asked for their own safer space. Together, Edel and Aaron created this space, which they tell us gives their students a voice, and gives them courage and confidence as young LGBT+ people. Aaron tells us that their club also impacts the wider school community, including parents, carers, and families.

It is promising to hear how well Edel and Aaron's group has been received by the wider school community. Parents, carers, and families are a vital part of the school community, and if we want to create truly LGBT+ inclusive educational spaces, they must be part of that. Many of our conversations demonstrate that DEI work is well received by the wider school community. This is sometimes referred to as the 'silent majority': the majority of parents, carers, and families who support LGBT+ inclusion, but aren't always actively vocal about their support.

While the silent majority do support LGBT+ inclusive educational spaces, we have heard a few stories of where this has gone wrong. It is useful to hear these stories because they contain important lessons on how we can get our connection with this vital part of our school communities right.

Andrew Moffat (S1, E7) is a teacher, leader, and the author of the resource 'No Outsiders: Everyone Different, Everyone Welcome'. Many of you will be familiar with at least parts of Andrew's story, and you can hear it in full in his episode. In our conversation, Andrew tells us about two occasions where his connection with the wider school community had broken down because of DEI work, and importantly what lessons these experiences taught him. One of these experiences resulted in the 2019 protests outside Andrew's school in Birmingham, which many of us saw on the national news at the time. At one point, Andrew describes to us being stood in his classroom but hearing hundreds of his wider school community outside chanting, 'Get Mr Moffat out!' Can you imagine how difficult that must have been? His description of this time is heart-breaking, but he does share with us three important lessons that he has learnt from this experience which can help us all to get our connection with the wider school community right.

First, Andrew tells us how these experiences made him move away from the word 'celebrate'. He tells us how this work gave the school community the perception that he was forcing all children to celebrate LGBT+ people, which simply was not the case. Andrew now uses the language of acceptance and respect, rather than celebration. He explains that if using the words accept and respect, rather than celebrate, can bring more of the wider community into the work, then it is a compromise worth making.

Second, Andrew tells us how his inclusion work began with the resource 'Challenging Homophobia in Primary Schools', which has now become 'No Outsiders'. No Outsiders is a more holistic approach to DEI. The resource is about accepting and respecting diversity more broadly than just LGBT+ identities. Again, Andrew tells us this more holistic view of inclusion helps to bring more of the wider school community into the work.

Finally, Andrew is very clear that some of the protests and community breakdowns that he has experienced have been due to a lack of clear consultation and communication. Andrew now advocates for schools to clearly consult with parents and communicate with them about the LGBT+ education happening. This ensures that the wider school community is aware of what is happening in school, and why it is happening. It also gives an opportunity for conversations before things become challenging.

This call for clear consultation and communication is mirrored in our conversation with Kyrstie Stubbs (S1, E8). Similarly to Andrew, Kyrstie tells us about challenges she faced in one of the schools she leads because she had not clearly consulted and communicated with the wider school community about the LGBT+ work her school was doing. Through conversations with parents, carers, and families, Kyrstie was able to bring them back on board with their work. She would explain to them The Equality Act and detail how she fights for all of those protected characteristics.

It is worth noting that both examples of challenges within the wider school community are in part due to the faith within that school community. We will discuss this in more detail in the next chapter.

What Andrew and Kyrstie's stories demonstrate is the importance of clear consultation and communication to aid connection with the wider school community in relation to LGBT+ inclusion work. To be clear, when I say consultation, I do not mean asking permission. LGBT+ inclusion work does not require permission, but through clear communication and consultation you can create the space for dialogue and discussion. You can create a space where your wider school community can bring any concerns or questions to you, rather than them escalating in private conversations you aren't a part of. In Chapter 4, we introduced the concept of a common inclusion goal. Specifically, we suggested: we want every person in our school communities to be free to be themselves, to feel seen, to feel safe, to feel supported, and to feel like they belong. This goal doesn't have to be something only agreed by staff, or by students, but it can also be agreed with the wider school community. If they have agreed to your common inclusion goal, it gives you a point of reference if you need to navigate challenging conversations with parents, carers, or families about the inclusion work happening in your school.

We hear how well this worked for Hannah (S1, E14) when she was working as the headteacher of a new start-up school. Hannah tells us that she established 12 values within her school, two of which were equality and diversity. She explains how all students, and their families, signed up to these values when they joined the school. These values were woven into the fabric of the school. They were visible in lessons, in assemblies, and throughout the school space. The school reward and sanction system were built around these values. With these values established as a common goal, Hannah was able to use them to navigate conversations with the wider school community.

I started this section by reflecting on how important community and connection are. Since then, we have heard how important they are to LGBT+ educators, to LGBT+ students, and explored how we can get our connection with the wider school community right. There is a lot to reflect on within this chapter. These stories demonstrate the value of community and connection, while also noting their complexities. One of the reasons for the complexities of our school communities is how diverse they often are. While this book focuses on the inclusion of LGBT+ identities in educational spaces, there are myriad other identities which we of course want to feel included. Our next chapter will consider this, as we explore intersectionality.

IN ACTION

Reflect on your school staff community.

How would an LGBT+ colleague feel supported and connected in your community?

Reflect on your student community.

How would LGBT+ young people feel supported and connected in your community?

Reflect on your wider school community.

Are you clearly consulting and communicating your common inclusion goal with the wider school community?

PODCAST EPISODES REFERENCED IN THIS CHAPTER

- Season 1, Episode 5 – B Guerriero

B (they/them) is a primary school teacher and LGBT+ youth worker with charity The Proud Trust. They join us to share their experience as a non-binary immigrant navigating a career in education.

- Season 2, Episode 2 – Helen Richardson

Helen Richardson (she/her) is a deputy headteacher and led the diversity network for her school's Trust. Helen joins us to share her experience growing up during Section 28, and now working as an out, lesbian educator.

- Season 2, Episode 4 – Edel Cronin & Aaron Brooks

Edel (she/her) is a vice principal and works alongside English teacher and Head of House Aaron (he/him). They join us to share their experience working together to run an LGBTQ+ club for students in their school.

- Season 1, Episode 14 – Hannah Wilson

Hannah (she/her) is a former headteacher, coach, trainer, and co-founder of Diverse Educators. She joins us to share her experience as an LGBT+ ally supporting Diversity, Equity, and Inclusion with Diverse Educators.

- Season 2, Episode 5 – Bennie Kara

Bennie (she/her) is a deputy headteacher, author, and co-founder of Diverse Educators. Bennie joins us to discuss her book, her role in Diverse Educators, and to reflect on intersectionality and her experiences as a gay Asian woman.

- Season 2, Episode 7 – Daniel Tomlinson-Gray

Daniel (he/him) is a secondary teacher and co-founder of LGBTed. He joins us to discuss the origins of LGBTed, and their book: *Big Gay Adventures in Education*.

- Season 2, Episode 12 – Nick Kitchener-Bentley

Nick (he/him) is a secondary school lead practitioner and teacher of drama, inclusion and English. He joins us to discuss his experiences, and how connecting with other LGBT+ educators can be transformational.

- Season 1, Episode 3 – Allison Zionts

Allison (she/her) is a secondary school teacher and PhD researcher exploring LGBTQ+ safe spaces. She joins us to discuss her research, and share her experience as a bisexual, Jewish woman.

- Season 1, Episode 12 – Adam Breslin

Adam (he/him) is a science teacher and PhD researcher exploring LGBT+ rights and activism in education. He joins us to discuss the power that every teacher, child, and young person has to change the world through gentle acts of activism.

- Season 1, Episode 4 – Dominic Arnall

Dominic (he/him) was the CEO of LGBT+ young people's charity 'Just Like Us' at the time we spoke. He joins us to discuss the great work that Just Like Us does to support LGBT+ young people and schools.

- Season 1, Episode 7 – Andrew Moffat

Andrew (he/him) is an Assistant Headteacher, and creator of the resource 'No Outsiders: Everyone Different, Everyone Welcome'. Andrew joins us to share the story of No Outsiders, and explore how we can bring the wider school community on board with DEI work in schools.

- Season 1, Episode 8 – Kyrstie Stubbs

Kyrstie (she/her) is an inspirational former headteacher, now Deputy CEO, and an LGBT+ ally. She joins us to share how her leadership approaches diversity, equity, and inclusion in a holistic, and meaningful way.

REFERENCES

Carlile, A., & Paechter, C. (2018). *LGBTQI Parented Families and Schools: Visibility, Representation, and Pride*. Routledge.

Educate & Celebrate. www.educateandcelebrate.org/

Just Like Us, Pride Groups. www.justlikeus.org/home/get-involved/pride-groups/

Meyer, I.H. (2003). Prejudice, social stress, and mental health in lesbian, gay, and bisexual populations: Conceptual issues and research evidence. *Psychological Bulletin, 129* (5), p. 674.

No Outsiders, No-outsiders. https://no-outsiders.com/

7

INTERSECTIONALITY

> *'What people don't often recognise is what people with an intersectional identity like mine bring to the table.'*
>
> *Bennie Kara*

IN THEORY

Use of the term 'intersectionality' has grown within diversity discourse to the point where a meaningful discussion about diversity and inclusion can't be had without it. Discussions of equality and inequality tend to discuss one protected characteristic at a time, but of course this is not how they are experienced. Intersectionality gives us a lens with which to examine how layers of inequality or disadvantage can often compound to create distinct and unique forms of discrimination against people with multiple protected characteristics. Perhaps a rather heavy start to a chapter, but intersectionality is a crucial concept and one that we need to understand to ensure LGBT+ inclusion is approached meaningfully.

Let's start with the origins of the term itself. Intersectionality was coined by Law Professor Kimberlé Crenshaw (1989) in response to a legal case in which Emma DeGraffenreid, an African-American woman, made a claim against a local car manufacturing plant for not hiring her on the grounds of her race and gender. Emma's claim was dismissed with the defence that the employer did hire African-Americans and did hire women. However, the issue was that all the African-American employees were men and completed manual labour, and all the female employees were white and completed secretarial work. Emma's claim was one of double discrimination, but as the court wouldn't allow her to put these two courses of action together, her claims were thrown out. Crenshaw talks about the origins of the term in her inspirational TED talk (2016) in which she explains that there wasn't a name for this 'discrimination squared' problem and that when there isn't a name for a problem, we can't see a problem, and therefore can't solve it. Crenshaw coined the term 'intersectionality' to name and address this problem; to reveal the multiple and intersecting ways power can operate to discriminate.

You may have heard or used the term 'intersectionality' before and be thinking this explanation doesn't quite line up with your understanding. Crenshaw acknowledges that use of the term has evolved over time to think about different forms of discrimination and privilege, recognising that intersectionality can be used as a lens to interrogate each of these. So, we could describe intersectionality as an analytical framework that allows us to examine how different aspects or layers of a person's identity can combine to create different forms of discrimination or advantage.

I said in Chapter 2 that I tend not to be seen as particularly remarkable in educational settings, and while I have shared experiences of discomfort in this book, you may notice that I haven't shared any experiences of overt discrimination. Examining this through the lens of intersectionality reveals that I am a very 'acceptable' and privileged LGBT+ person. I'm a gay, white, middle-class, able-bodied, cisgender male, in a monogamous relationship. If we flip these descriptors, we might consider how different my experience would be. If I were a bisexual, black, working-class, disabled, trans woman in a polyamorous relationship, it's likely I would experience many forms of oppression and discrimination at the same time, such as racism, transphobia, and monosexism. It's also unlikely I would be intelligible in a school as many of these identities are rarely seen in educational settings. Crenshaw explains the issue with Emma's case was one of framing, as the court had no pre-existing schema to understand the discrimination she had faced (we will return to this later). Audre Lorde (1982) famously said there is no such thing as a single-issue struggle because we do not live single-issue lives. I love this quote and think it is a beautiful way to highlight the need for intersectional approaches to LGBT+ inclusion.

We've touched upon a few examples, but let's take some time to think about the different layers of identity that could potentially intersect with LGBT+. The nine protected characteristics of The Equality Act (2010) are a good starting point. The Equality Act stipulates that it is against the law to discriminate against anyone because of:

- age;
- gender reassignment;
- being married or in a civil partnership;
- being pregnant or on maternity leave;
- disability;
- race including colour, nationality, ethnic or national origin;
- religion or belief;
- sex;
- sexual orientation.

We could also think about characteristics not covered by The Equality Act that may lead to discrimination, such as socio-economic background or body size. I would encourage a moment of reflection here, perhaps with a pen and paper, to think about the different types of discrimination LGBT+ people may experience. I'd then encourage you to think about how these challenges could become more difficult with the intersection of other characteristics. In doing this exercise, you may think about discrimination you have experienced yourself, or discrimination you have seen other people experience. It may be that you struggle to relate to any of these protected characteristics, providing an equally useful opportunity to examine your experience of privilege. It is also worth considering how discrimination may feature later in your life as you gain protected characteristics, for example marriage or civil partnership, maternity or paternity, age, or even disability. At this point, I would encourage putting down the book and spending some time with these thoughts.

How did you find that exercise? You might have thought about the challenges LGBT+ young people from religious backgrounds face in trying to explore their identity while remaining part of their family and culture. You may have thought about loopholes in The Equality Act that allow single sex schools to discriminate against trans students on the basis of sex. You might have thought about the barriers that result in women and people of colour being underrepresented in senior leadership, considering how this may make career progression even harder for a Black, gay woman. You might have thought about the challenges of same-sex parents negotiating equitable maternity/paternity rights with their employer. You might have thought of other examples, or you might have struggled to think of any, and that is absolutely fine. What we are hopefully doing in this chapter and in this book is what we need to do in schools. We need to make space for open discussion, and to listen to the multi-experience lives of our students and colleagues so we can become better teachers and allies. An aspect of The Equality Act that people are often less aware of that is helpful to point out, is that you are also protected from discrimination if:

- you're associated with someone who has a protected characteristic, for example a family member or friend;
- you've complained about discrimination or supported someone else's claim.

This section of the Act is useful to share with colleagues and students as it reminds us that we should be championing and supporting those around us and that good allyship is about standing side-by-side with those with lived experiences different to our own, as we will explore in the final chapter.

I would now like to return to Crenshaw's notion of pre-existing schemas. Schema is a word I'm sure most teachers are familiar with thanks to the increasing appetite for cognitive science within education. A schema describes a pattern of thought or behaviour that organises categories of information and the relationships between them. When Crenshaw explained that the issue with Emma DeGraffenreid's case was one of framing, what she meant was that the courts didn't have a pre-existing schema that linked the ways racism and sexism could intersect for a black woman to experience multiple forms of discrimination. When schemas are talked about in school, they are usually done so with reference to what students already know, and consequently, the most efficient way in order to teach them something new. This cognitive science approach to teaching and learning is something we also need to be aware of as we plan inclusion within our curriculum. We need to understand our students' current schemas about LGBT+ people and plan opportunities to develop them further.

Earlier, I asked us to think about the multiple forms of discrimination I may experience as a bisexual, black, working-class, disabled, trans woman in a polyamorous relationship. My description may have felt on the cusp of comedic, due to the sheer number of minority identities that I had described. It may have also felt abstract due to the lack of schema we have for what this person may look like. Let's strip this example back even further. Hopefully, our colleagues and students will have schemas that allow them to understand the lives and experiences of a range of LGBT+ people, but it's also important to understand where the gaps may be. How many of our students would have a pre-existing schema which allows them to picture what a Black trans woman may look like and what some of the challenges she may face are? Or a disabled bisexual man? Or a Muslim non-binary person? This idea of pre-existing schema goes back to our discussion in Chapter 5 about the importance of the curriculum acting as windows, allowing students to look through and learn about lives different to their own. When we are planning our curriculums, we need to usualise a broad and intersectional range of lives so our students have empathetic and realistic understandings of the challenges and opportunities that different members of the LGBT+ community may experience.

I hope this chapter provides a useful opportunity to think about privilege and discrimination, and how these intersect with LGBT+ identities. As teachers, we have wide circles of influence and the opportunity to change hearts and minds every day. With the right curriculum and classroom culture, we can provide platforms that centre the voices of marginalised people, ensuring their experiences are seen and heard. In the spirit of centring marginalised voices, I would like to finish this section by returning to Audre Lorde's Harvard University speech.

> The 60s for me was a time of promise and excitement, but the 60s was also a time of isolation and frustration from within. It often felt like I was working and raising my children in a vacuum, and that it was my own fault – if I was only Blacker, things would be fine. It was a time of much wasted energy, and I was often in a lot of pain. Either I denied or chose between various aspects of my identity, or my work and my Blackness would be unacceptable. As a Black lesbian mother in an interracial marriage, there was usually some part of me guaranteed to offend everybody's comfortable prejudices of who I should be. That is how I learned that if I didn't define myself for myself, I would be crunched into other people's fantasies for me and eaten alive. My poetry, my life, my work, my energies for struggle were not acceptable unless I pretended to match somebody else's norm. I learned that not only couldn't I succeed at that game, but the energy needed for that masquerade would be lost to my work. And there were babies to raise, students to teach.
>
> (Lorde 1982)

IN PRACTICE

When I try to conceptualise intersectionality, I think about the bay window in my parents' house (okay, this might not be how you expected that sentence to end, but go with me on this...). Each year when it is my Mum's birthday that bay window is filled with cards wishing her a happy and healthy birthday. There are cards addressed to Mandy, Mum, Grandma, Daughter, Wife, Neighbour, Sister-in-law, and friend. All different identities, but all one person, they are all my Mum.

None of us are one thing alone, but instead a combination of identities that overlap, interplay, and intersect. If we want to create truly LGBT+ inclusive educational spaces, we must consider this intersectionality. The inclusion of LGBT+ people without the inclusion of disabled people, people of colour, neurodivergent people, or people of faith is not LGBT+ inclusion – because LGBT+ people could be any of those things additional to their LGBT+ identity. Let's hear how intersectionality plays out in the lives of some of our podcast guests.

In Chapter 3 we introduced you to the honorary third member of the Pride & Progress team, George White (S1, E2). George is an example of where LGBT+ identities intersect with faith. He is a trans man, and a Catholic. He is an LGBT+ activist, and a teacher of Religious Education in a Catholic school. George tells us how he has experienced some friction around this intersection. At one point in our conversation, I ask George how he brings together his Catholicism and his trans identity. The way George answers my question reveals my own ignorance. The lack of representation I had experienced had limited the development of my schema. In my mind, these two things were distinct and different – but George explains that in his life, they are not. George tells us that on numerous occasions he gets asked if he can be transgender and an RE teacher. He answers, 'I'm standing right in front of them – so of course, the answer is yes'. Our conversation with George is a great example of how faith can intersect with LGBT+ identity, but also highlights how this intersection can at times create friction.

In the previous chapter, we saw how this friction became challenging for Andrew (S1, E7) and Kyrstie (S1, E8). The reality is that all these statements are true: some people of faith feel a religious fiction with LGBT+ identities; some people of faith are LGBT+ people themselves; and importantly, we are required to make our educational spaces inclusive for both LGBT+ people and for people of faith.

So, how do we bring these truths together? Our conversation about Andrew and Kyrstie's experiences hold the answer to this: using legislation as a safety net, we make it clear that we stand with all protected characteristics including faith and LGBT+ identities; we focus on acceptance and respect of all people; and we ensure there is clear consultation and communication around the inclusion work we do. Schools should not shy away or be quiet about the inclusion work they are doing; this silence creates space for misunderstanding. Be open and clear about your inclusion work, explaining why it is not only a legal requirement of you as an educator, but also a moral duty. As we discussed in the previous chapter, establishing that common inclusion goal is a great safety net to fall back on if we come up against these tensions.

Another intersection we have explored regularly on the podcast is the intersection between a person's LGBT+ identity, and their race, ethnicity, or nationality. You will remember B Guerriero (S1, E5), the primary school teacher and LGBT+ youth worker who is non-binary. In Chapter 3 we shared some of the challenges B has faced as a non-binary person, but they also tell us that being an immigrant has previously presented a bigger challenge than being LGBT+. 'Being an immigrant is not an easy thing', they tell us, 'making my way into the world of education was tricky, because people have prejudices and biases.' B's story is a great example of how existing at the intersection of two marginalised identities can result in accumulating barriers, inequalities, or challenges.

The challenges B shares with us come from outside of their community and are rooted in peoples' bias or prejudice. But we have also heard that having an intersectional identity can lead to challenges from within your community. Denise Henry (NEU LGBT+ Educators' Conference Special) is the Black executive seat holder for the NEU, meaning she represents black members' voices within the union. We caught up with her as part of our special episode covering the NEU LGBT+ Educators' Conference 2022. During our conversation, Denise talks to us about the intersection of being a Black, lesbian woman. She explains how this intersection has caused friction from some people within the Black community. However, she is now seeing big changes as people come to know her better and become more accepting of all of her identity. Denise feels that people are no longer judging her identity, but instead judging her only on the quality of the work she is doing to represent them. Denise tells us how important it has been for her to hold both parts of her identity and to see some members of her community change their mindset.

While it should not be their responsibility to do so, it is common for us to hear of people with intersectional identities changing mindsets. Many people have very limited perceptions of what a lesbian, gay, bisexual, or transgender person may look like – and people whose LGBT+ identities intersect with other identities can challenge these perceptions. You will remember Karan (S1, E6) from Chapter 1. Karan is a science teacher and a gay man who grew up in India. In our conversation, we discuss the responsibility Karan feels to be a role model of both a gay man, and an Indian man. He explains that he feels he must let his students know that you can be Indian and gay. He hopes that his presence in school is helping students to shift their mind and challenge the limited views they may have of what a gay man looks like.

The ability to change mindsets, or challenge limited perceptions is very powerful. In our conversation with Bennie (S2, E5), she suggests many people don't recognise these advantages, which people who have intersectional identities like hers hold. We introduced Bennie earlier as the co-founder of Diverse Educators, but she is also a deputy headteacher who specialises in curriculum, teaching, and learning. There was a lot to discuss in our conversation with Bennie, but we spent time exploring her intersectional identity as a gay, Asian woman. Bennie explains that people often make assumptions about her sexuality, assuming that because she is Asian, she could not be gay. She explains some of the systemic barriers against her, how she experiences multiple microaggressions, and the emotional tax of this combination. While Bennie is very aware of the inequalities that currently come with her identity, she also recognises the power she has as a visible gay Asian person. She argues we need to recognise the benefits and the strengths that people who have grown up with intersectional identities may have developed, including: increased empathy, deep curiosity, and a strength for inclusive leadership.

Bennie's reflections are a perfect way to end this chapter. She is clear that the way the world perceives her intersectional identity results in barriers, inequalities, and challenges. Yet, she recognises the power and opportunity that her identity gives her. This model of hope rather than deficit is a powerful lens to approach intersectionality with. One of the strengths Bennie has seen in educators with intersectional identities is their inclusive leadership. We will explore how, and why, LGBT+ people may make great leaders in our next chapter which focuses on school leadership.

Before we move into the 'In Action' reflections for this chapter, we want to acknowledge that as educators, we believe there is always room for further learning, and further growth – that is as much true for us as it is for anybody reading this book. There is, of course, space for Pride & Progress as a platform to learn, grow, and do better. This section has explored the intersections between LGBT+ identities and religion, and that between LGBT+ identities and race. However, writing this chapter has also highlighted several other important intersections which our podcast is yet to explore in detail. While we are proud of the diversity showcased in our work, we will be looking for ways to amplify the voices of an even more diverse range of intersectional identities as we move forwards.

IN ACTION

Google search 'The Wheel of Power and Privilege'.

Look at the diagram and reflect on your own experiences.

In which areas of your identity do you have power and privilege, and are there areas in which you might experience marginalisation?

(Continued)

Repeat this reflection from the perspective of your students.

Reflect on the visibility of intersectional identities in your school.

How can you further help students to develop schemas for a broad and diverse range of identities?

Reflect on the strengths of intersectional identities.

How can you celebrate intersectional identities, and recognise the many benefits and strengths that come from having a diverse and intersectional school community?

PODCAST EPISODES REFERENCED IN THIS CHAPTER

- Season 1, Episode 2 – George White

George (he/him) is a teacher of Religious Education, inclusion leader, and LGBTQ+ inclusion consultant. He joins us to share his experience as a trans man now teaching in the same Catholic school he attended as a student.

- Season 1, Episode 7 – Andrew Moffat

Andrew (he/him) is an Assistant Headteacher, and creator of the resource 'No Outsiders: Everyone Different, Everyone Welcome'. Andrew joins us to share the story of No Outsiders, and explore how we can bring the wider school community on board with DEI work in schools.

- Season 1, Episode 8 – Kyrstie Stubbs

Kyrstie (she/her) is an inspirational former headteacher, now Deputy CEO, and an LGBT+ ally. She joins us to share how her leadership approaches diversity, equity, and inclusion in a holistic, and meaningful way.

- Season 1, Episode 5 – B Guerriero

B (they/them) is a primary school teacher, LGBT+ youth worker, and a trustee of the UK Literacy Association. They join us to share their experience as a non-binary immigrant navigating a career in education.

- Special Episode – NEU LGBT+ Educators' Conference

In this episode the hosts of Pride & Progress capture the NEU's LGBT+ Educators' Conference 2022, where the conference theme was 'Defending our Community'. During this episode you can hear from Just Like Us, Olly Pike, Schools Out UK, Stonewall, Trans Actual, Kacey De Gruit, Denise Henry, and Divina De Campo.

- Season 1, Episode 6 – Karan Bhumbla

Karan (he/him) is a secondary school science teacher. He joins us to share his experience as a gay, Indian science teacher working to be a positive representation for all facets of his identity.

- Season 2, Episode 5 – Bennie Kara

Bennie (she/her) is a deputy headteacher, author, and co-founder of Diverse Educators. Bennie joins us to discuss her book, her role in Diverse Educators, and to reflect on intersectionality and her experiences as a gay Asian woman.

REFERENCES

Crenshaw, K. (1989). Demarginalizing the Intersection of Race and Sex: A Black Feminist Critique of Antidiscrimination Doctrine, Feminist Theory and Antiracist Politics. U. Chi. Legal F. 139. https://scholarship.law.columbia.edu/faculty_scholarship/3007

Crenshaw, K. (2016). Kimberlé Crenshaw: The urgency of intersectionality | TED Talk. Available at: www.ted.com/talks/kimberle_crenshaw_the_urgency_of_intersectionality

Government Equalities Office (2010). Equality Act 2010: guidance. www.gov.uk/guidance/equality-act-2010-guidance

Lorde, A. (1982). Learning from the 60s. www.blackpast.org/african-american-history/1982-audre-lorde-learning-60s/

8
LEADERSHIP

'When you've got somebody at the top of the organisation who is proudly themselves, they give everybody else permission to be themselves as well.'

Professor Catherine Lee

IN THEORY

As a business teacher of 15 years, I've spent a lot of my career discussing leadership. My first question to students is usually 'what's the difference between a manager and a leader?'. It's a question they find hard to answer and one that generates interesting discussion. Spend a minute thinking about it yourself – it's quite hard to define, isn't it? While there tends to be some overlap, definitions for managers generally involve executing the day-to-day running of an organisation, perhaps with a certain rigidity and set of expectations. Leaders, on the other hand, are centred on vision and ensuring staff are empowered and enabled to drive change that achieves an overarching goal. A fairly reductive summary of management and leadership, especially from a business teacher, but a helpful starting point to think about what leadership is and its role within a school.

My second question to students is the one we're going to think about in this chapter: what makes a good leader? This is often a divisive question, especially when discussed in the context of politics. Thankfully, we're going to steer clear of that topic and keep the focus on what makes a good school leader and how good school leaders can champion LGBT+ inclusion. Depending on your position in a school, you are going to have a different perspective on this chapter, so we should start by thinking about who a leader within a school is. The most obvious person is the headteacher; the person who sets the vision, ethos, and culture for the school – but who else? Don't the governors have the ultimate say in the direction of the school? What about the rest of the senior leadership team? Middle leadership? Aren't teachers leaders within their classrooms, too? Yes, would be the short answer to these questions – all of these people have the ability to influence and steer culture, meaning all of us have leadership potential within a school.

Leithwood et al. (2008) argue that school leadership has a greater influence on schools and pupils when it is widely distributed, suggesting the impact a headteacher can have on pupil learning alone is minimal (typically 5–7%), but when leadership and staff work collaboratively, this percentage can increase five-fold. This chapter will allow you to think about how you can work collaboratively with leadership teams, as well as develop your own leadership, to make LGBT+ inclusion a priority.

A headteacher isn't meant to be an expert in every area of school, in the same way a Prime Minister or President isn't meant to be an expert in every area of governing – this is why they are surrounded by experts and advisors. The job of a leader is to recognise what is important, identify key priorities and then mobilise the right people to ensure these priorities are achieved. Often, one of the biggest barriers to LGBT+ inclusion within a school can be the senior leadership team. Now, I'm not naïve – I understand why LGBT+ inclusion often isn't a priority within schools. Headteachers have a phenomenal amount of responsibility and are constantly dealing with new challenges and demands. The education system is so heavily focussed on pupil progress and attainment, it's easy to see how LGBT+ inclusion can slip down the list of priorities.

This is where we come in. In reading this book or listening to the podcast, you are acutely aware of the need for LGBT+ inclusion. In reaching out and working collaboratively with our leadership teams, we stand to make an impact beyond our classrooms. I've always been of the mindset that you shouldn't go to senior leaders with problems without also offering solutions. This means they are less likely to fob you off and are more likely to commit to action. The first step in getting leadership teams to understand the importance of LGBT+ inclusion is getting them to recognise there is a problem. Sharing the findings from Stonewall or Just Like Us' research is a good starting point to highlight headline issues such as bullying and anxiety (or for the most results-driven leadership teams, highlighting the negative impacts these have on engagement and progress). An even better approach is getting senior leaders to talk with LGBT+ staff or pupils from the school.

I recently did some training for a group of senior leaders in a Trust, both primary and secondary, in which I shared my story as well as some of the Stonewall data and stories from the podcast. Most of the leaders had never considered the inherent cis/heteronormativity of their schools and were genuinely surprised to hear how difficult LGBT+ people can find these spaces. Many of the leaders acknowledged that they had assumed that things 'were fine' these days. A week after the session, I received an email from a headteacher who told me that he had bought a pride pin to wear on his lanyard. He said a student had come up to him the next day and asked him why he was wearing it, to which he explained about the training he had attended and how he wanted to do more as a leader and ally. The child had then felt comfortable enough to tell him that he was bisexual, and after chatting about his experience, invited the headteacher to the lunchtime pride club. The headteacher described how emotional and humbled he had felt in attending the group, explaining that he had no idea so many students attended and how important it was for them. He said it had opened his eyes and given him the confidence and determination to prioritise LGBT+ inclusion within his school.

Sinek (2016) argues there are two things great leaders need: empathy and perspective. If we can help develop these two attributes in our leaders, it can lead to transformational change in our schools, as demonstrated by this example. Sinek beautifully explains that being a leader isn't about being in charge; it's about taking care of the people in your charge. It might be easy to think some school leaders don't care about LGBT+ inclusion, but it may just be that they don't know how to take care of their LGBT+ people. So, once we've got leaders to empathise and recognise there's a need for LGBT+ inclusion, what's next? In the spirit of providing solutions rather than problems, here are some things you or your leadership teams may begin by thinking about.

- Leaders don't need to be experts, but they can listen to understand. Leaders that recognise their limitations and work towards doing better are well respected by staff. Leaders can set up groups that give LGBT+ staff and students a platform and voice to share their experiences of what school is like – both positive and areas for development.
- Making a governor an LGBT+ or DEI lead is an impactful way of ensuring that LGBT+ inclusion remains a priority and is discussed on a regular agenda in the same breath as exam results and Ofsted. It also provides a platform to share feedback from the meetings.

- Ethos and culture need to be regularly communicated and should underpin everything that happens in a school. Leaders need to develop a common language, ensuring all members of a school know which words should and shouldn't be used. School culture should be palpable – values need to be lived, not laminated.
- Middle leaders can conduct curriculum scrutinies to identify where and how LGBT+ lives are included within the curriculum. Is representation intersectional? Where are the gaps and opportunities?
- Policies and procedures need to make explicit reference to LGBT+ people. This includes equality policies, mission statements, parent/student agreements, bullying policies, etc. Every school should also have a specific trans policy that has considered all aspects of school life from the perspective of a trans student or staff member.
- Ensure systems are inclusive. Is there a separate boy/girl uniform? Are there appropriate boxes on forms for LGBT+ parented families? Is there an opportunity for teachers applying to the school to share their gender, pronouns, and preferred teacher title? Can toilets be made gender-neutral? Are there safer spaces?
- Make LGBT+ lives visible. Are there displays with LGBT+ terminology and role models? Can staff wear pride lanyards? Is sharing pronouns usualised? Do LGBT+ staff feel supported to be visible?
- How is the wider community made to feel part of the school's inclusive culture? Some parents may have concerns or fears about LGBT+ inclusion and need support or education themselves.

This is far from an exhaustive list but begins a discussion about the role of leadership in LGBT+ inclusion. At the start of the chapter, I said getting leaders to recognise the importance of LGBT+ inclusion is often the biggest barrier. Having an LGBT+ member of staff work alongside leadership teams, or even better, on the leadership team, can help ensure this work is being done in an authentic and meaningful way. Now we're not suggesting that staff should be promoted to senior leadership simply because they're LGBT+, but good leaders need to recognise that teachers from minority groups often have a unique set of skills.

Catherine Lee's excellent article 'Why LGBT Teachers May Make Exceptional School Leaders' (2020) describes five skills beneficial to leadership that LGBT+ teachers often develop throughout their career. Catherine argues these attributes are acquired as a necessity to navigate the often challenging cis/heteronormative environment of school. The five attributes are reading people; compassion and commitment to the inclusion of others; making connections; managing uncertainty;

and courage and risk-taking. Catherine also identifies that LGBT+ teachers often avoid leadership roles for the fear that the status will necessitate greater personal scrutiny by school stakeholders. Schools that recognise the value of their LGBT+ teachers may find, with the right support and culture, that they are sitting on leaders with potential waiting to be unleashed.

In Chapter 6, I told a story about the headteacher who told me that he didn't care about people's sexuality and that he treated everyone the same. This rankled because what he was really saying was, 'as long as the job gets done, I don't care'. In A Level business we teach Blake Mouton's managerial grid (1964) which suggests five leadership styles, based upon two variables: concern for people and concern for results. If you google Blake Mouton and look at images, you will be able to see this grid. The theory suggests there is no one perfect leadership style and that different styles are needed for different environments. Approaches that have a high concern for results and a low concern for people are named authoritarian or 'produce or perish' leadership. Similarly, leadership that has a high concern for people but a low concern for results is described as 'country club' leadership (think Michael Scott in the US *The Office*). While these approaches may work in certain fields of industry, I'm sure we can all agree that education is as much about people as it is about results, if not more so. In which case, concern for both people and results need to be high, necessitating a 'team leadership' approach to ensure people feel valued and therefore able to achieve.

Schools are about people. When leaders develop empathy for the people in their charge, specifically the LGBT+ people in their charge, schools become more safe, inclusive, and productive environments for everyone.

IN PRACTICE

Early in my teaching career I applied for a master's programme at the University of Oxford. In writing this paragraph I considered pretending it had always been an aspiration of mine to attend such a prestigious institution – a lie I am certain I wrote in my application for the programme – but the truth is sadly more ridiculous. At the time of applying, I was in love with a guy who attended the University. My application was a combined effort to both impress him, and potentially gain the opportunity to see him more regularly. It was essentially the storyline of the first 30 minutes of the movie *Legally Blonde*, except somehow simultaneously more gay and less camp.

My initial intentions set aside, I was offered a place and thrilled to accept. When I started the course, it felt a little like leading a double life. I could be sat one day in a seminar room of the oldest university in the English-speaking world surrounded by academics, and the very next day on the playground of a small school in an area of high deprivation trying to support a single parent who was struggling to find the money to feed her children. It was a stark contrast – and what surprised me at the time, was how easily I adapted to function in both spaces.

It wasn't until we spoke with Catherine Lee (S2, E6) that I realised why I found that so easy – I had been doing it my whole life. As a queer person who grew up in a cis/heteronormative and religious environment, I learnt from a young age how to read the room, adapt my scripts accordingly, and perform in that space. This huge challenge in my teenage years was now a great strength which was helping me as an adult. This is precisely Catherine's argument, as presented by Adam earlier in this chapter. The adverse experiences of many LGBT+ people as a minority group can provide a range of skills which when recognised and harnessed can contribute to them becoming effective school leaders. Catherine now leads the Courageous Leaders programme: a mentor programme for LGBT+ people in educational leadership. She believes strongly that having LGBT+ people proudly at the top of an organisation gives everybody else permission to be themselves, and to be open and honest.

We can see what this looks like in practice through great LGBT+ leaders like Troy Jenkinson (S1, E13), who is a primary school headteacher and a gay man. In our conversation, Troy tells us that he believes we can get the most out of our teams when we truly know them. When he first started as a headteacher he met with every member of staff to get to know them. Through these conversations, he was honest about his own identity, and he found that as a result his team were honest in return. His authenticity created a space where all his team felt they could be open and honest, and every person could be themselves. In just this one example you can see how some of the attributes outlined in Catherine's research benefit Troy's leadership: compassion and commitment to the inclusion of others, reading people, and making connections.

In our conversation with leader Edel Cronin (S2, E4) she shares how she includes a rainbow flag on her presentations to leaders and governors in her role as leader of outcomes. Here she is subtly reminding staff that as well as being a leader, she is a queer woman, and that identities matter. Again, showing compassion and commitment to the inclusion of others.

While it is promising to read that LGBT+ people can make great leaders, it is equally hopeful to note that any person can be a great leader for LGBT+ people. In this book, we have introduced Hannah Wilson (S1, E14) as the co-founder of Diverse Educators, and as a former headteacher of a new start-up school. Hannah is also a leadership and development consultant, coach, and trainer. I first interacted with Hannah through Twitter where her username is @ethical_leader. Her Twitter handle is incredibly accurate – Hannah is an ethical leader, and DEI is at the heart of much of her work. Hannah argues that, while DEI work is the responsibility of every adult in a school, there should be a person who leads in this area. However, she recognises the extra time, responsibility, and energy that this work requires if it is to be done properly. Too often, people are asked to lead on this in addition to their workload as a bolt on, or because they have a visible protected characteristic. Hannah argues that the person leading on DEI in a school should be given additional time for the role, and financially compensated for the additional responsibility. She likens it to the role of the Designated Safeguarding Lead, or Special Educational Needs Coordinators in school. A leader like Hannah would give time to DEI, which would in turn empower those in her team to see it as a priority.

Another fantastic example of leadership in practice is Kyrstie Stubbs (S1, E8). Throughout this book, we have returned several times to our conversation with Kyrstie and in Chapter 2 we referred to it as a masterclass in inclusive leadership. There is much to learn from how Kyrstie leads empathy first.

Kyrstie begins our conversation by explaining that she sees it as her moral duty to educate children for the world in which they live. She recognises her privilege and wants to use that position wisely to ensure that every child and every staff member feels safe and part of her school community. Kyrstie comments that there are nine protected characteristics, and that leaders do not have the right to prioritise any of them or choose which ones to ensure are included in their school.

She explains some of the steps she has taken as a leader to ensure LGBT+ people are protected under her leadership. First, she ensured all her team understood the vision of LGBT+ inclusion. She did this by inviting an LGBT+ person to speak to her team, to help them to build empathy, and understands the importance of getting inclusion right. Kyrstie describes this experience as 'transformational' for her team. They were so deeply moved by the lived experiences of a trans woman, that every member of the team understood the vision and why it mattered. This action attaches a real person to a label which people may have preconceived ideas about and is a great first step to build empathy. From this, she then co-constructed a common inclusive language with her team in the way we described in Chapter 4.

Kyrstie's inclusive leadership doesn't just end with her team; she wants every person involved in the school community to understand her vision. To help achieve this she has clear statements about inclusion on her school website, and she asks every visitor to sign a statement which shows all of the protected characteristics and explains why these are important in her school.

Kyrstie's example of inclusive leadership is a demonstration of everything we have discussed in this book so far. She is aware of our current context in education, and of her moral duty as a leader. She actively challenges cis/heteronormativity using representation, visibility, and a purposefully designed curriculum. She has established a common goal, with a common inclusive language, and communicates with her community to ensure they are connected with it. Kyrstie is powerfully reimagining her educational space as an LGBT+ inclusive space in a way we can all learn from. If you are a leader, or aspire to be one, then please do listen to our conversation with Kyrstie.

Adam wisely started this chapter by explaining how all of us have the potential for leadership, and that any person working in a school will be a leader in some capacity. After hearing what this may look like in practice from some inspirational leaders, take some time to reflect on your own leadership and how it can be shaped to become more inclusive.

IN ACTION

If you are an LGBT+ person.

What skills might your experiences have given you which could help you in your role, or in future roles you aspire to one day be in?

If you are not an LGBT+ person.

How could you show allyship in your leadership, and help to create a more inclusive space?

Whoever you are, whatever your role.

How can creating and leading a school culture of inclusion benefit everybody in your school community?

PODCAST EPISODES REFERENCED IN THIS CHAPTER

- Season 2, Episode 6 – Professor Catherine Lee

Catherine (she/her) was a PE teacher before stepping into academia at Anglia Ruskin University. She joins us to discuss her experience as a lesbian PE teacher during Section 28, her current research into LGBT+ leadership, and setting up the Courageous Leaders programme.

- Season 1, Episode 13 – Troy Jenkinson

Troy (he/him) is a primary school headteacher and children's book author. He joins us to share his experience as an early career teacher during Section 28, and now as an inclusive leader.

- Season 2, Episode 4 – Edel Cronin & Aaron Brooks

Edel (she/her) is a vice principal and works alongside English teacher and Head of House Aaron (he/him). They join us to share their experience working together to run an LGBTQ+ club for students in their school.

- Season 1, Episode 14 – Hannah Wilson

Hannah (she/her) is a former headteacher, coach, trainer, and co-founder of Diverse Educators. She joins us to share her experience as an LGBT+ ally supporting Diversity, Equity, and Inclusion with Diverse Educators.

- Season 1, Episode 8 – Kyrstie Stubbs

Kyrstie (she/her) is an inspirational former headteacher, now Deputy CEO, and an LGBT+ ally. She joins us to share how her leadership approaches diversity, equity, and inclusion in a holistic, and meaningful way.

REFERENCES

Blake, R., & Mouton, J. (1964). *The Managerial Grid: The key to leadership excellence.* Gulf Publishing Company.

Lee, C. (2020). Why LGBT Teachers May Make Exceptional School Leaders. www.frontiersin.org/articles/10.3389/fsoc.2020.00050/full

Leithwood, K., Harris, A., & Hopkins, D. (2008). Seven strong claims about successful school leadership. *School Leadership and Management, 28*(1), pp. 27–42.

Sinek, S. (2016). Most Leaders Don't Even Know the Game They're In. www.youtube.com/watch?v=RyTQ5-SQYTo

9

IDENTITY

'This is it. This is who I am. I still struggle with a great sense of shame… but fundamentally I am who I am… I don't deny my existence.'

Claire Birkenshaw

IN THEORY

Before I trained to be a teacher, I was a teaching assistant in a PRU (pupil referral unit) for a year. Although 24, I had the babyface of a 14-year-old and was conscious of how I was perceived next to all the 'proper' teachers. I felt like an imposter among the staff; anxiously feeling I didn't look the part and constantly worrying I wouldn't be taken seriously.

The PRU was small and at lunch time we would eat with the students. One day, a student came in with a new pair of glasses, and for fun, the staff tried them on one at a time, while the students gleefully provided their reviews. When it came to my turn to try the glasses on, one of the students exclaimed, 'Wow, they make you look like a teacher!'. Only months from teacher training, and mindful of my youthful exterior, this passing comment had a huge impact – these students thought I looked like a teacher! So pleased was I to be seen as 'what a teacher should look like', that the next weekend I went to the opticians for an eye test, in the bizarre hope I would need glasses. (At the risk of losing the moral of the story, it turns out my eyesight was appalling, and that I should have been prescribed glasses years earlier – I have my vanity and that student to thank for my current optical health!)

Joking aside, the point I'm making is that we all enter educational spaces with a preconceived idea of what a teacher should look and act like, and often use this as a blueprint to perform an expected role. As we've already explored, most people's educational template was constructed during a time when LGBT+ inclusion was either limited or non-existent. Consequently, teachers often feel the need to perform the expectations of cisgender heterosexuality (even if they are), in turn, making others feel they must do the same. This chapter will examine the concept of identity from the perspective of both teachers and students, exploring the challenges and opportunities of being open and authentic.

Identities are not fixed. Throughout our lives, our personal and professional identities evolve and change, continually influenced by a myriad of factors. The intention of this chapter is not to explore arguments of nature versus nurture, but to think about the aspects of our identities that feel true and authentic to us. Goffman's (1959) concept of *dramaturgy* is an interesting framework to employ here, to explore the ways we as teachers may perform an identity – or as Goffman describes, perform 'impression management'. Goffman argues that everyday social life is like a theatre, in which we are all actors who perform roles that we have been socialised into. Goffman suggests we use scripts, props, costumes, and gestures to communicate a particular impression, and that 'the self' is made real through our performance and interaction with others. Comparing teaching to being an actor on a stage may feel like a leap, but if we think about the ways teachers explicitly (teacher training) and implicitly (the staff room) learn what it is to be a teacher, we may begin to identify the ways we are performing an expected role. Thinking about ourselves in this way may feel existentially challenging – are we performing the role of a teacher in a way that is authentic to us, or are we just performing it in a way that we've been socialised into and is therefore expected of us?

This question becomes even more challenging when explored from the perspective of LGBT+ teachers. If schools are spaces where being cisgender and heterosexual are silently assumed, we as LGBT+ teachers are left with an impossible dilemma: should we be inauthentic and lie about who we are, or should we come out and fear discrimination? It's certainly not a decision we've been prepared for in teacher training, nor one we make just at the start of our careers; it's a decision we make with every class, with every colleague, and in every school in which we work. As LGBT+ teachers, we must decide whether to remain silent and invisible, or to put ourselves under a metaphorical spotlight. Patai's (1992) description of 'surplus visibility' helps us conceptualise what this metaphorical spotlight may look like. Surplus visibility refers to the attention, warranted or not, that a member of a minority group attracts. This visibility can then create a shift in public perception where the individual may be perceived to accurately represent the entire minority group, providing an unjustified and unachievable level of responsibility. It also means LGBT+ people's identities can become 'extrapolated from part to whole', where this single aspect becomes the defining feature of their identity. In schools, where sexuality and gender are simultaneously assumed yet considered inappropriate topics for discussion, you can imagine the strain this puts on teachers who are defined by theirs.

For LGBT+ teachers who feel it is easier to conceal their identity to avoid this spotlight, the effects can also be harmful. Building upon Goffman's dramaturgy analogy, Hochschild (2010) considers the role of emotion within impression management, specifically in the workplace. Hochschild suggests that employees need to develop 'emotional labour', meaning they need to manage their feelings in line with the rules and expectations of the workplace. Extending Goffman's acting metaphor, Hochschild argues that emotional labour results in either 'deep acting' or 'surface acting'. Deep acting refers to employees drawing upon emotions they believe to be authentic and appropriate to the workplace; surface acting describes employees displaying emotions which are inauthentic but expected of the workplace. Hochschild argues that workers who feel obliged to be inauthentic regularly may experience self-estrangement or distress. Both LGBT+ students and teachers who are unable to be their authentic selves in schools often find themselves surface acting, and literally performing a role inauthentic to them. When I think back to the start of my career, huge amounts of my energy were consumed by concealment and surface acting because I felt unable to share or explore my authentic identity.

I have used Goffman, Hochschild and Patai's work to try and illustrate the ways in which LGBT+ teachers often feel the need to perform an identity that fits an expected role. I also use them to highlight the damaging effects of concealment, surface acting and inauthenticity, especially over time. If you aren't LGBT+, you may still find it interesting to use Goffman and Hochschild's ideas to reflect on the way you perform the role of a teacher. Are there parts of your role that feel like surface acting? Are you employing props, clothes, scripts, and behaviours that feel inauthentic to you? Where do your personal and professional identities overlap?

So far, we've explored the concept of identity from the perspective of teachers – we will now think about this from the viewpoint of our students. We could argue that impression management is even more important for the young people in our schools. Our students are in a perpetual state of exploring and developing their identities, all while trying to fit in and be liked. They are trying to find the clothes, props, language, gestures, and scripts that feel authentic to them. As Goffman argues, these aspects of identity are only validated or made real by interaction with others. The challenge being, of course, that the peers offering this validation are experiencing the exact same process of experimentation and desire for endorsement. It's no wonder every kid in my school thought Kappa popper tracksuit bottoms were the height of fashion for non-uniform days in the 90s. (If you're not old enough to know of the sartorial horror to which I refer, please take a moment to google them, while saying a prayer for my generation.)

School is such a crucial time for development, and so it is vitally important we are creating spaces where students can safely explore their identities and not feel the need to conceal or deny who they are. I spend a lot of time visiting schools and it's encouraging to see the increasing number of LGBT+ students who can be open and authentic about their identities. Sadly, this is not the case everywhere, but it does highlight that when this work is done well, and the right culture is created, something truly special can happen. As we said at the start of the book, we are at a unique and pivotal time for inclusive education, where schools for the first time ever are being strongly encouraged and enabled to become LGBT+ inclusive. My hope is that schools that choose not to prioritise this work will soon look like they're on the wrong side of history. For too long, young people have had to put their identities on hold until they are in a safe enough space to unfold. Encouragingly, it does appear that we are on the cusp of a generational tidal shift, where identities are being explored and described in new and exciting ways.

In 2023, the Office for National Statistics released their 2021 LGBT+ census data. The results showed that over 1.5 million people in England and Wales identified as LGB+, with 262,000 identifying their gender as different to the one they were assigned at birth. The demographic breakdown wasn't available at the time of printing, but Stonewall's recent and hopeful *Rainbow Britain Report* (2022) demonstrates a clear trend in the decreasing number of people identifying exclusively as heterosexual. For Baby Boomers (as of 2022, ages 56–75), 91% identified as heterosexual; for Gen X (43–56), 87%; Millennials (27–42), 82%; and Gen Z (16–26), 71%. As with all statistics, this data can be interpreted and analysed in a number of ways, but the trend does tell a compelling story. Institutions that aren't developing culture, curriculum, language, visibility, or leadership that embraces LGBT+ lives may soon be looked upon as an anachronism. In recent training, I have found this a convincing line of argument (coupled with Ofsted and The Equality Act) to get leaders to take this work seriously. Once schools realise their current practices aren't inclusive of a generation who increasingly identify their gender and sexuality in new ways, an appreciation and sense of urgency for this work is quickly developed.

Schools don't want to find themselves in a position where their students are more knowledgeable, open-minded, and socially aware than their staff.

Throughout this chapter, you may have thought about the other themes in this book and how they overlap with the topic of identity. In many ways, the previous chapters have outlined the conditions that are required to allow, not just LGBT+ people, but all people to authentically flourish in a school. The more that staff and students feel safely able to explore their identities, the greater permission it gives to those around them. This is particularly true of the LGBT+ staff in our schools. In a recent paper, I argued that LGBT+ teachers in supportive environments may have access to new and empowering forms of visibility. This visibility can help destabilise the cis/heteronormativity that permeates and restricts all people within a school. I argue that rather than surplus visibility, LGBT+ teachers may have access to powerful visibility (Brett 2022). I use Young's (2009) concept of *powerful knowledge*, describing knowledge which enables students to think beyond the current limits of their own understanding and experience, to conceptualise the impact visible LGBT+ role models can have. If LGBT+ teachers and students can conceive of their identity as something powerful, something that expands understanding and empathy, and something that develops better well-being and mental health for them and those around them, the impact could be truly significant.

IN PRACTICE

There is a picture I often show when I am delivering training in schools. I'm looking at that picture now. It shows a young teacher, they must be new to the profession. They're wearing a dark-blue, formal shirt, their short freshly faded hair perfectly in place, held out of their eyes by a pair of brown, round glasses. There is a child on either side of them smiling – maybe laughing – as they all look down at what is being shown on the iPad screen held in the teacher's hands. It is the kind of picture you might see in an advertisement for teacher training, or the prospectus of a school.

In fact, that is exactly what it is. The photograph was taken for an educational advertisement. The iPad wasn't even switched on, and the only reason the children are smiling is because the photographer had said 'right, everyone laugh and pretend your teacher said something really funny'.

I know this because I am the young teacher in the photograph – although most people don't realise that even as I stand in front of them side-by-side with the image. I don't blame them. Truthfully, I don't recognise the person in that photo at all.

The purpose of the 'In Practice' sections of this book is to share with you the lived experiences of our podcast guests to demonstrate what the discussion Adam has set out about this theme looks like in practice. In this chapter, I want to do things slightly differently and share with you my own story: the story of the first time I shared my identity in the classroom.

Like Adam, when I entered the profession, I was conscious of wanting to look like a teacher. I had grown up in a system which was not inclusive, a system where LGBT+ people were silenced in schools, and this impacted what I imagined a teacher could be. Before starting my PGCE, I bought suits I would never normally choose to wear, cut my long hair short, and started to prepare the way I wanted to present in my new role. Goffman's dramaturgy would suggest I was preparing my scripts, props, costumes, and gestures ready to engage in impression management. As I entered the profession, I was actively trying every day to look like a teacher, dress like one, talk like one, and fit in as one. I thought I knew what a teacher had to look like, and I was trying desperately to fit that mould.

As a result, I was lying every day. Or as Hochschild would suggest, I was surface acting. I was hiding parts of myself in a way which was exhausting, just as we discovered it was for Troy, Catherine, and Shaun at the beginning of this book. At that point, I had never really considered how my personal identity might interplay with my new professional identity, but the fact they were seemingly forced to be kept separate was increasingly difficult.

This continued for a few years, until one day those two identities came crashing together. I was teaching Year 6 at the time. A child, who was angry at a decision I had made in class, stood up and shouted homophobic comments to me before running out of the classroom. After ensuring the child was safely with an adult who could help regulate their anger and keep them safe, I returned to a classroom of 30 children staring at me. They were waiting to see how I was going to respond.

Honestly, I didn't know what to say. After all, there is no PGCE seminar on what to say when a child outs you publicly. Initially, I considered just moving on, brushing past it, and continuing with the lesson I was teaching. It certainly would have been the easiest option to just move on. But, in that moment standing at the front of a curious class, I realised how loud my silence would be. I'd heard that sound before – my whole childhood had been surrounded by it.

I remembered what it felt like to hear discrimination met by silence. I remembered being 10 years old knowing that I was different and beginning to learn that difference was wrong. There was something wrong with me. I knew it because I never saw anybody like me. Not in the books we read in class, the adults that surrounded me, or the films we watched when it rained at break time. There was something wrong with me. I knew it, because I heard boys talk about girlfriends and girls talk about boyfriends and I knew that wasn't what I wanted. The boys were encouraged to do 'boy things' and the girls grouped together to do 'girl things' and I floated in between not really belonging anywhere.

I first learnt the words that I would later identify with used as insults to attack people like me. The same words were later used to attack me directly, and later still they became words I used to attack myself. All of which, for the most part, went unchallenged. All of which, for the most part, was met with silence.

So, back in my Year 6 classroom where I stood now at the front of the class as a teacher. I couldn't allow that cycle of silence, becoming shame, becoming silence again, to continue. So, I took a deep breath, and I shared my identity with my class for the first time.

The conversation that followed was brilliant. My class, as children so often are, were empathetic and kind. Some of them had LGBT+ relatives who they talked about, and they helped the other young people in the room to understand some words which were new to them. We explored how some of the words that young person had used were not inherently wrong, but the way he had weaponised them were.

When the conversation came to an end my teaching assistant took over for a moment while I excused myself. I walked down the corridor to the staff room, closed the door behind me, and I broke down crying.

I cried that day because after years of hearing those words used as weapons it still hurt to experience that. I cried because I once again felt like I was having to reveal myself as though I was something that should be hidden in the first place. But, most of all, I cried because I felt like I had just done something important. In that moment I had broken a cycle of silence and shame. I couldn't imagine how much it would have changed my life if somebody had been able to do that for me when I was a child.

That day changed my life. My personal and professional identity came together for the first time, and a weight was lifted. I stopped surface acting and started reading from a script that was true to me. That day started a long process of me learning the power of being myself authentically in the classroom – a process which has led me to be writing this book with Adam.

I wanted to share that story with you to demonstrate a few points. First, to demonstrate further what Goffman and Hochschild's theories look like in practice. To show how the separation of a teacher's personal and professional identity can cause damage. The concealment of who I was made me feel inauthentic, it was an emotional labour which prevented me from being the best teacher I could be. Second, to show how damaging it can be for a young person to grow up in a space where their identity isn't safe. My school did not allow space for my identity, and it resulted in me feeling different, alone, and like I did not belong. Finally, to show how powerful it can be when we create an opportunity for personal and professional identity to come together. Now, I get to do work that I love. I get to host conversations about diversity, help school staff to reimagine their educational spaces as equitable and inclusive, and spend time writing this book. Sometimes I find it hard to believe that all of this was on the other side of that door which for years people told me not to open. All of this is only possible because of the parts of my identity which I spent years trying to hide.

When I became a teacher, my personal identity had to make room for my new professional identity and at the time I was not encouraged to explore how they might overlap. As a result, I found myself in a challenging situation which I was unsure how to navigate. I don't want any other educator to be in the same position, or to feel they must be inauthentic in the classroom. Consequently, Adam and I have been working with a lot of early career teachers (ECTs) exploring the relationship between personal and professional identity. We often do an activity with them to help them explore what this looks like in practice for them. The activity goes as follows:

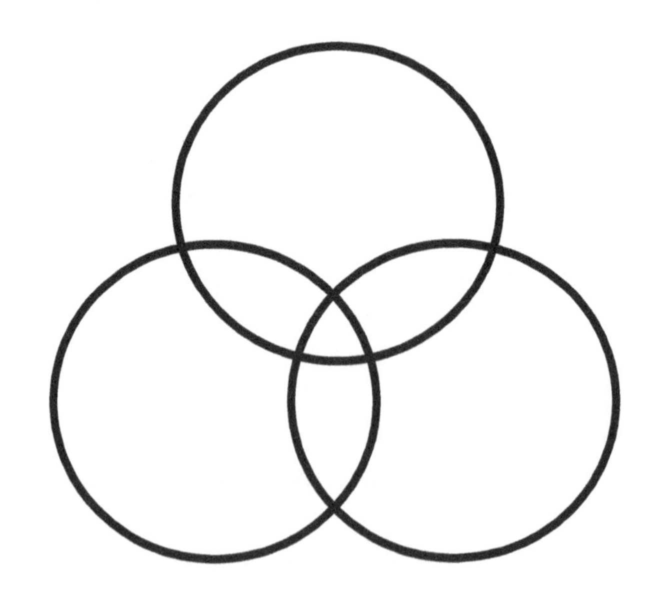

1. Draw three circles, overlapping as a Venn diagram.
2. Label those three circles:
   - Personal Identity (home you)
   - Teacher Identity (classroom you)
   - Colleague Identity (staff room you)
3. Begin to populate these circles, considering who you want to be in each space, and where these things intersect and interrelate.

This activity helps teachers to make conscious decisions about their identities. For me personally, my identity as a queer non-binary person must be in the centre intersection. I need that part of me to be free in any space I occupy. However, I choose not to share any information about my romantic relationships in the schools I work in. That is the professional choice, which is right for me, but may not be the choice which is right for everybody. We should all be free to draw these professional lines for ourselves, in a way which feels right for us.

For an LGBT+ person, it is not unprofessional for them to share their identity in the educational spaces they occupy, or to talk about their partner, spouse, or family. In fact, there are powerful lessons in these conversations, and they should be empowered and enabled to have them if they choose to. However, it is not a requirement for them to do so. To keep their personal identity separate is also professional and absolutely fine if that is the choice which supports them. Our schools need authenticity, they need diversity, and they need teachers who show young people that difference is strength. But our identities are exactly that, ours. Teachers should be free to choose for themselves how much of their identity they choose to share with this profession.

That being said, it is worrying how many ECTs I speak to who are unsure if their personal and professional identities are allowed to intersect. I have spoken to lesbian women who still change the pronouns of their partner in the classroom because they aren't sure if they are allowed to say they live with a woman, and non-binary people who use titles in school which make them uncomfortable because they feel that they have to. As we explored in Chapter 1, we are still being tripped up by the cycle of silence and shame which remains rooted in our educational spaces. Many LGBT+ educators still feel unsure about their freedom to be authentic in educational spaces, particularly at the beginning of their career.

Charlotte Feather (S2, E10) is a trained primary school teacher, now working as an academic tutor at the University of Sunderland. She is a researcher, and the founder of the brilliant LGBTQ+ Primary Hub: a website set up to help create inclusive environments for all children. Her research, which we discuss during the episode, looks specifically at the professional identities of LGBT+ ECTs. Three key themes emerged from her research: preventable barriers, the role of communities, and freedom to exist as a queer teacher. She argues that we need to reimagine our schools as places where teachers can be the authors of their own stories, be surrounded by a supportive community, and have the freedom to share their personal identities if they choose to.

Ultimately, the discussion around identity presented in this chapter goes back to the common inclusion goal we discussed earlier: we want every person in our school community to be free to be themselves, feel seen, feel safe, feel supported, and feel like they belong. If we all believe this statement should be true, then we must consider how we make space for all identities in our school community.

IN ACTION

Reflect on Goffman's concept of dramaturgy.

Are you able to be authentic in your role as an educator?

Are you employing clothes, props, and scripts which feel authentic to you?

Have you consciously constructed professional boundaries which feel right for you?

Reflect on the educational space you are creating.

Have you created an environment in which students feel comfortable to explore, develop and share their identities?

Reflect on the concept of powerful visibility.

How can you empower students and colleagues from minority groups to see their differences as a source of strength and opportunity?

PODCAST EPISODES REFERENCED IN THIS CHAPTER

- Season 1, Episode 16 – Dr Adam Brett & Jo Brassington

The creators of Pride & Progress are joined by special friend of the show George White to reflect on the first season of the show, and to discuss what is to come next.

- Season 2, Episode 10 – Charlotte Feather

Charlotte (she/her) is an educator, researcher, and the founder of the LGBTQ+ Primary Hub. She joins us to discuss her experience growing up as a bisexual woman in a rural area, and her research into the experiences of LGBTQ+ early career teachers.

REFERENCES

Brett, A. (2022). Under the spotlight: Exploring the challenges and opportunities of being a visible LGBT+ teacher. *Sex Education*, 1–15. 10.1080/14681811.2022.2143344

Goffman, E. (1959). *The Presentation of Self in Everyday Life*. Doubleday.

Hochschild, A. R. (2010). The managed heart: Commercialization of human feeling. *The Production of Reality: Essays and Readings on Social Interaction*, 320À336.

Office for National Statistics. (2023). *Sexual Orientation, England and Wales Census 2021*.

Patai, D. (1992). Minority status and the stigma of 'surplus visibility'. *The Education Digest*, *57*, p. 35.

Stonewall. (2022). *Rainbow Britain Report*. www.stonewall.org.uk/resources/rain-bow-britain-report-2022

Young, M. (2009). Education, globalisation and the 'voice of knowledge'. *Null*, *22*(3): 193–204. 10.1080/13639080902957848

10

ALLYSHIP AND ADVOCACY

> *'I am not a diverse educator – I am an ally to diverse educators… being seen and heard is a privilege that I had which I took for granted in my own schooling and I want to make sure that I'm part of the solution rather than part of the problem moving forwards.'*
>
> Hannah Wilson

IN THEORY

Allyship and advocacy are at the beating heart of Pride & Progress and so it feels only right for us to conclude the book with this important theme. We're also aware that the concepts of allyship and advocacy sometimes cause unease as they can sound either intimidating or unattainable. In this chapter, we aim to take away that fear, dispel the myths, and think about what allyship looks like in day-to-day practice. When I think about allyship, I think of the adage 'a ship in the harbour is safe, but that is not what ships are built for'. Reading this book is a superb act of allyship and we hope it has developed your confidence and understanding of LGBT+ issues. We now want to help you develop your advocacy and take these ideas to sea.

A question I often get asked in training is 'why do LGBT+ people need straight/cis allies?'. I don't begrudge this question as I understand where it is coming from – partly from a sense that there is already an LGBT+ community of support, and partly because LGBT+ inclusion has already come such a long way. While both are true, there are many compelling answers to this question.

Because we are a minority.
Because LGBT+ hate crimes are on the rise.
Because LGBT+ people are underrepresented in positions of power.
Because LGBT+ people are often spoken on behalf of.
Because Anti-LGBT+ legislation exists in countries all around the world (including the UK).
Because LGBT+ people are more likely to experience negative mental health.
Because transphobia is becoming the new homophobia.
Because schools remain unsafe places for LGBT+ people.

LGBT+ people need allies because there remains work to be done. Now the good news is that anyone can be an ally – in fact you don't even need to describe yourself as an ally. Many respected DEI leaders believe allyship is something that should be described of us through our acts, and not a badge we award ourselves. I love this framing as it keeps the focus on our actions and not the accolade.

> Allies are individuals who are members of a privileged social group who support and advocate for members of an oppressed group.
>
> (Washington & Evans 1991)

For social change to take place, allyship is required. Washington and Evans' use of the word 'advocate' allows us to conceptualise allyship as a verb rather than a noun, where action is required to affect change. Keeping the focus on action rather than the language of allyship is a powerful way to approach this work with our staff and students. We also need to be aware that developing people's confidence and skill takes time and that we are not going to make our school population LGBT+ advocates overnight. We must also recognise that acts of advocacy begin with small steps and need to begin with the individual. Claire Bale, a DEI lead for a large Trust and good friend, has written a superb blog (link in the references) called The Circle of Influence (2020) in which she explores the initial steps we can all take on our allyship journey.

Now 'journey' is a word that often makes me cringe, but in the context of LGBT+ inclusion, it is an appropriate one for us to uncurl our toes and use. Nobody is an expert in all areas of LGBT+ inclusion – including us. There are always new things to learn and there isn't a knowledge finishing line you get to cross where you are awarded a rainbow medal (sadly). The most powerful thing we can do with our staff and students is to get them to recognise their starting points and support them on the next steps of their journey.

Brown's ally continuum (2018) is a superb tool (you can google the model) to highlight the different stages a person may go through on their allyship journey, spanning from apathetic to advocate. She describes the following four stages:

1. Apathetic: No understanding of the issue
2. Aware: Knows basic concepts, not active on behalf of self or others
3. Active: Well informed, sharing and seeking diversity when asked/prompted
4. Advocate: Committed, routinely and proactively championing inclusion

This is a brilliant self-assessment tool that I use in training to ask delegates, without judgement, to consider their current position and to then make a personal pledge about how they will progress further. This exercise has the most impact if you tell people they don't need to share the information and that it is purely for them. In my experience, this task often leads to open and honest conversations where people don't feel guilty for their current position but feel motivated to do better. Brown discusses the continuum and how it can be used in an excellent episode of The Will to Change podcast, the link to which can be found in the references.

Brown's continuum brings allyship to life by replacing passivity with the language of action and intent; without action, it's easy to fall into the trap of performative allyship. There is no better example of this than the 2022 Qatar World Cup where celebrities like Robbie Williams and David Beckham, who have spoken of their support of the LGBT+ community, and brands like Coca-Cola and McDonald's, who adopt the rainbow colours every Pride month, accepted huge sums of money to endorse a country with shocking anti-LGBT+ laws. These people and companies were happy to be seen as LGBT+ allies when it financially benefited them, but once acts of advocacy or activism were required, the limits of their allyship were quickly revealed.

In recent years, I have seen many educational institutions, particularly universities, adopt rainbow lanyards or have 'pride crossings' painted on their grounds. These are wonderful acts of visibility, but without action, can be considered at best, performative, and at worst, harmful. If a member of staff is wearing a pride lanyard, they are communicating that they are a safe person to talk to. If the colleague hasn't taken the action necessary to develop the language or knowledge that is required to support an LGBT+ student or colleague who may go to them for help, the distress caused could be significant. Institutions need to ensure that their claims of allyship are emblematic of the LGBT+ work they do and are not simply a marketing facade. While of course nowhere near as egregious as the Qatar example, this does highlight the need for claims of allyship to be met with action.

In a blog for Stonewall, Hobson (2017) shares five useful tips for those who want to ensure their allyship is attributed to action. Two of these tips, 'discover the challenges facing the LGBT+ community today' and 'get involved in the community and show your support', provide a useful opportunity for us to unpack the LGBT+ initialism once again. Throughout the book, we've highlighted the great progress that some members of the LGBT+ community have benefited from, but the key word here is 'some'. Dozens of countries around the world still have anti-LGBT+ laws, and even progressive countries continue to demonise specific members of the LGBT+ community. In the UK, transphobia currently feels frighteningly like the homophobia of the 1980s that led to Section 28, not helped by a government who refused to include trans conversion therapy in a 2022 law banning other forms of LGBT+ conversion therapy. Florida's controversial 'Don't Say Gay' bill is another example highlighting how quickly moral panic can lead to legal restriction and public vilification.

As a member of the community who has benefited from much of the progress we have described, I am acutely aware of the need for allyship, and this motivates me to advocate for the rights of others. For example, I am not a trans person, but I can advocate for my trans siblings and try to use my privilege and position to leverage support. This includes simple things like keeping up to date with legislation and public discourse, signing petitions and attending rallies, reading books about trans lives, and challenging systems in school that aren't inclusive of trans and non-binary people. These are relatively small actions but are each an act of solidarity that speaks up for trans lives and advocates for their rights and inclusion. I also wear a trans pride lanyard to demonstrate my support and as a symbol that I am a safe person to speak to.

It's not just laws and legislation we need to be aware of; there are many identities within the LGBT+ community that still face discrimination. The inclusion and acceptance of people like myself is sadly not always experienced by other members of the community, particularly identities that challenge the rigid binary of our society. It is up to us to call out comments or actions that discriminate and to challenge systems designed to exclude, which leads us to the final point on Hobson's list – 'stand up for what you believe in'. I started the chapter by using the analogy of a ship in a harbour. You may currently be reading this book sitting in the staff room, lying on the sofa, or relaxing in a coffee shop, nodding along with everything Jo and I say, and generally being a fabulous ally. The challenge for us all is remaining as committed to LGBT+ inclusion when we leave the harbour and are met by storms.

It's easy to imagine that when you come across discrimination or hateful language you will whir into action, righting wrongs and effortlessly challenging the behaviour and views of people speaking and acting in a hurtful manner. The reality can be very different and truthfully, sometimes standing up against

> discrimination can be an intimidating experience. The important thing is to let your voice be heard and although it's not always easy, these are situations where being an ally really counts. It's important to let those with bigoted views know that they are not in a world where they can marginalise or bully those that need our support – and this is really the essence of what being an ally is all about.
>
> (Hobson 2017)

This quote captures what I'm sure we have all experienced before – wanting to challenge discrimination but not quite being sure how to go about it. The first thing to say is, don't give yourself a hard time if you don't contest every view you disagree with, or if you don't deal with every situation perfectly. It can take time to build up the confidence and vocabulary needed to effectively call out unacceptable behaviour, but it is the effort and intent that is important. I want to share with you a superb acronym that my friend Shonagh Reid (2022) uses in her DEI consultancy which provides a scaffold for challenging discrimination. The acronym is IDEA: interrupt, describe, explain, and apology/action. Let's have a go at applying Shonagh's model by imagining that we are walking past a student at lunch time in the dining hall using homophobic language. The series of actions could look like this:

- Interrupt: 'Can I stop you there, please'
- Describe: 'I just heard you use the word faggot'
- Explain: 'This is homophobic language and is not tolerated in this school; do you understand why this is such an offensive term?'
- Action: 'I will be recording this as a homophobic incident and reporting it to...'
- Apology: 'I only want you to apologise when you understand why this isn't okay'

Every situation will of course be different, and what we say and when we say it may differ, but the model provides a structure to describe and deal with behaviours that, crucially, lead to action. The above example shows how we might deal with a student using a 'calling out' approach; however, the model can also be helpful in addressing staff. Challenging the behaviour of a colleague is of course difficult, particularly if they are more senior, and this is where a 'calling in' approach may be better suited. Calling in means a conversation is had privately, likely after the event. The stages are just as important, but the conversation is likely to have a greater emphasis on the explaining stage, where you identify why what took place made you feel uncomfortable or wasn't acceptable. In most instances, when a colleague understands why their actions were inappropriate, the result is in an apology and commitment to do better. In the hopefully unlikely event that this isn't the result, or that you feel further action is required, you should speak to an appropriate leader, governor, or union rep, about how the situation can be escalated further.

Calling out behaviour is hard and so it's worth briefly returning to the topic of emotional labour from the last chapter. It is important that we practise self-care when advocating for ourselves or others. LGBT+ inclusion can be sensitive and triggering work that comes with an emotional tax, and so it is important we look after ourselves and only complete this work when we feel safe and supported to do so. Don't forget what we said in Chapter 6 about community – there is a huge network of colleagues out there to support you and provide guidance and advice, and that includes Jo and I.

As we've explored, while advocacy and allyship can provide challenges, developing these skills in our staff and students is the ultimate way to make our schools LGBT+ inclusive. Best of all, there is a body of research that highlights the many benefits of being an ally. Rostosky et al. (2015) argue that allies develop knowledge and awareness that satisfies relationships and community belonging, as well a sense of meaning and purpose that we get from actively contributing to social change. These benefits contribute to important psychological well-being not just for us, but also for the people who we advocate for. While we don't do this work for our own gain, it's a wonderful feeling to know that our advocacy and allyship benefits ourselves as well as everyone around us, contributing to making schools safe and inclusive spaces for everyone.

IN PRACTICE

A lot of my contribution to this book was written in coffee shops in Manchester, where I live. Partly because I find it easier to work outside of the house, but mostly because I treat people watching as somewhat of a hobby. There is one spot I am particularly fond of, and I came here today to write this chapter.

I arrived half an hour ago and went to use the toilet before I sat down to write. There are two bathrooms, and today there was quite a long queue. I stood waiting for some time, as one of the bathrooms remained locked and we all took our turn using the other.

Eventually, I took my turn. As I was heading to my seat to begin writing this chapter, I noticed a person walk over to the bathroom that had been locked since I arrived. I watched as they tried the handle, and to my surprise the door opened right away. The person that tried the handle seemed content as they locked the door behind them, while those who had been standing in the queue for some time looked less pleased.

The cubicle had been unoccupied the entire time, the door had always been open, and any of us could have walked right through it if we had only tried to.

Why didn't I try the handle myself, I wondered? Since arriving, everybody around me had acted like it was locked, and some people explicitly told me it was. I had learnt from the people around me that I should not try to open the door.

As I watched the queue slowly deplete and reflected on the title of this chapter, I considered a parallel with this situation and the power of allyship. As a young person, I remained 'in the closet' for so long – waiting on one side of a door because I believed I couldn't ever be on the other side. Everybody around me acted like the door was locked, and some people told me directly to not try and open it. The actions of other people made me feel like I didn't have permission. But when I finally built up the courage to try the handle – when I finally decided to come out of the closet – I learnt that the door had been open the entire time. Not only that, but what was beyond that door was exactly what I had been waiting for and needing all along.

Now, imagine how much sooner I would have tried that handle if the people around me hadn't been silently acting like I could never do it, if they had told me that was an option, if their actions had given me permission. This is why allyship and advocacy are so important – we are social creatures and the actions of those around us impact us. Young LGBT+ people need to grow up with allies around them who don't limit them, who allow them to try the handle, whose actions give them permission to find exactly what they need on the other side of the door.

But what does allyship look like in practice? In our podcast we have spoken to LGBT+ educators about the importance of allyship, as well as speaking with brilliant allies themselves. Let's hear what a few of them had to say about allyship and advocacy in practice.

We began this chapter with a quote from Hannah Wilson (S1, E14). I recently heard a colleague describe Hannah as the embodiment of allyship, and as I listen back to our conversation, I see how they landed on that description. In her episode, Hannah explains that she is herself a white, straight, able-bodied, cisgender woman. Yet, her work through Diverse Educators has done so much to support marginalised people who do not carry the same privilege. The key here is that Hannah is aware of that privilege. She tells us that she grew up with the privilege of being seen, being heard, and feeling belonging. In her work now, she wants to do what she can to ensure more people can have that same experience of belonging. In her words, she is working to 'be part of the solution rather than part of the problem moving forward'.

Hannah explains that allyship is about humanity. It is about disrupting cycles of discrimination not as a performative act to look good, but instead because it is the right, human thing to do. She explains to us that this allyship must begin with listening and learning. In a later conversation we speak with Hannah's co-founder of Diverse Educators, Bennie Kara (S2, E5). Building on Hannah's starting point of listening and learning, Bennie also reminds us that this process must simultaneously involve unlearning. Like Destin on the backwards bike (see Chapter 3), we must learn and unlearn in unison to discover a new way of doing things. In education, we so often recycle ideas, or continue to do things because it is the way we have always done them. Bennie argues we have to question these cycles of habit by taking a real, honest look at our current ways of thinking, by noticing our bias, and seeing where unlearning is necessary. Together, Hannah and Bennie suggest that our starting point as allies is doing the work to listen, learn, and unlearn.

This work may take different forms. For some of our guests, this has come through reading: an approach you have chosen by reading this book. There is an increasing library of literature that can help you to understand LGBT+ peoples' lived experiences, our history, and the barriers and inequalities that challenge us. For others, this work comes in the form of a podcast, as many of you will have chosen when you listen to Pride & Progress. Powerfully, some people choose to connect directly with LGBT+ people and invite them into their school to share their lived experience. We have spoken previously about the transformational power of stories making space to hear people's stories. There are several ways that listening, learning, and unlearning can be approached – but whichever approach you choose, connecting with and listening to the lived experiences of LGBT+ people is the starting point of LGBT+ allyship.

In our conversations with Hannah and Bennie, they then explain to us how listening, learning, and unlearning must be followed with a commitment to action. Adam has already discussed this commitment and outlined what some of those actions might look like. By this point in the book you should have a long list of possible ways your allyship or advocacy might begin to take shape.

As Adam has suggested, the words allyship, advocacy, or activism can seem daunting. When I first started reading these words, I imagined protests and placards. I thought of the household names who have fought for the rights we all enjoy today, and I believed my own actions could never compare to theirs. One of those household names, Peter Tatchell (S2, E14), joined us on the podcast to discuss his life's work. Peter has been campaigning for human rights, democracy, LGBT+ freedom and global justice for over 50 years. Inspired by the Black Civil Rights Movement, Peter's activism began in 1967. Among his many involvements, he was a leading activist in the Gay Liberation Front from 1971–74 helping to organise the first London Pride in 1972, and later he was involved in the queer human rights direct action group OutRage! from 1990–2011. Now, through the Peter Tatchell Foundation, he continues to campaign for human rights in Britain and internationally.

Our conversation with Peter is a fascinating lesson in LGBT+ history. His tone strikes a perfect balance between the recognition of how far we have come, with acute awareness of how far we still have to go. You can learn more about Peter's life-long commitment to advocacy and activism by listening to his episode, or further still by watching the documentary 'Hating Peter Tatchell', available on Netflix. In the documentary, Stephen Fry explains how Peter 'deserves recognition for his extraordinary contribution to the happiness of millions who have never heard of him'. Peter's life, his advocacy and action are exactly as Stephen suggests – extraordinary – but not everyone's has to be.

Before speaking with Peter, I admit I felt a little intimidated by his extraordinary achievements. I was then surprised when he ended our interview by thanking us for the work that we do. Peter Tatchell thanking us? Our small acts of advocacy could never compare to his. But Peter explained that with advocacy, 'it is a collective effort. It is you, me, and all of us. It is we together. That is how change happens.'

Of course, he is right. Change happens because of all our actions – some bigger, some seemingly smaller. We explore this in our conversation with Adam Breslin (S1, E12), who is an A-Level biology teacher, and a PhD researcher focusing on LGBT+ rights and activism in education. Our conversation focuses on exploring the idea of teachers as activists. Adam explains to us that while activism is a word that frightens some people, at its root it simply means being an agent of change. He explains how this is scalable in a way that we can all engage with – and small everyday activism can be powerful.

In reflecting on our conversations with Hannah, Bennie, Peter, Adam, and many others, I have come to see the value of all our actions of allyship and advocacy – no matter their size. Some of my own advocacy and activism feels small, like wearing an AIDS HIV awareness red ribbon on my coat. Other actions feel bigger, like coming to the end of writing this book. Each action, big or small, holds value.

I have come to think of much of my work as diluted activism. When we dilute something, yes, we make it weaker, but we also increase its capacity. My small acts of diluted activism aren't all strong, but they have the capacity to reach all the spaces that I occupy. When we dilute activism, we make it something that all of us can engage with, and we therefore increase its capacity to stretch further and wider. As Peter says, 'that's how change happens'.

IN ACTION

Reflect on Brown's ally continuum: apathetic, aware, active, advocate.

Where do you feel your allyship lies on this continuum? Where would you like it to be?

Reflect on what you have heard throughout this book, and the role of listening, learning, and unlearning.

What have you learnt? What unlearning have you had to do? Have you experienced any discomfort in the process?

In this final chapter, as you take the time to reflect on what you have learnt and unlearnt, we encourage you to specifically look back over the In Action prompts in each chapter. As you do so, reflect on how your knowledge and commitment towards creating LGBT+ inclusive educational spaces has changed since reading this book.

While these ideas are fresh in your mind, we suggest committing to some short-term, medium-term, and long-term actions.

What will your allyship and advocacy look like after reading this book?

How will you actively reimagine your educational space as more LGBT+ inclusive? What further support do you need to make this happen?

PODCAST EPISODES REFERENCED IN THIS CHAPTER

- Season 1, Episode 14 – Hannah Wilson

Hannah (she/her) is a former headteacher, coach, trainer, and co-founder of Diverse Educators. She joins us to share her experience as an LGBT+ ally supporting Diversity, Equity, and Inclusion with Diverse Educators.

- Season 2, Episode 5 – Bennie Kara

Bennie (she/her) is a deputy headteacher, author, and co-founder of Diverse Educators. Bennie joins us to discuss her book, her role in Diverse Educators, and to reflect on intersectionality and her experiences as a gay Asian woman.

- Season 2, Episode 14 – Peter Tatchell

Peter (he/him) has dedicated his life to campaigning for human rights and has been involved in LGBT+ activism for over 50 years. He joins us to share his life experience fighting for equity.

- Season 1, Episode 12 – Adam Breslin

Adam (he/him) is a science teacher and PhD researcher exploring LGBT+ rights and activism in education. He joins us to discuss the power that every teacher, child, and young person has to change the world through gentle acts of activism.

REFERENCES

Amos, Christopher. (2021). *Hating Peter Tatchell*. [Documentary]. Netflix. Retrieved from: www.netflix.com/title/81422831

Bale, C. (2020). The circle of… influence. thatsabitracey.com/2020/10/03/the-circle-of-influence

Brown, J. (2018). The Will To Change: Uncovering True Stories of Diversity & Inclusion: Minisode #14: From Unaware To Accomplice: The Ally Continuum willtochange.libsyn.com/minisode-14-from-unawareto-accomplice-the-ally-continuum

Hobson, J. (2017). Come Out For LGBT: Becoming an active LGBT ally. www.stonewall.org.uk/about-us/news/come-out-lgbt-becoming-active-lgbt-ally

Reid, S. (2022). IDEA: A Framework For Challenging Discrimination in the Moment. shonaghreid.com/blog/f/idea-a-framework-for-challenging-discrimination-in-the-moment

Rostosky, S. S., Black, W. W., Riggle, E. D., & Rosenkrantz, D. (2015). Positive aspects of being a heterosexual ally to lesbian, gay, bisexual and transgender (LGBT) people. *American Journal of Orthopsychiatry, 85*(4), p. 331.

Washington, J., & Evans, N. J. (1991). *Becoming an ally. Beyond Tolerance: Gays, Lesbians, and Bisexuals on Campus*. American Coll. Personnel Association, pp. 195–204.

CONCLUSION

> *'Don't accept the world as it is. Dream of what the world could be – and then help make it happen.'*
>
> *Peter Tatchell*

Peter's quote feels like the perfect call to action on which to end. When we first sat down to discuss writing this book, we set a mission statement that we wanted to educate, inspire, and provide teachers with the strategies they need to make their classrooms more inclusive and equitable. After reading this book we hope you feel we have achieved that.

The book began with an overview of the historical and current challenges facing LGBT+ inclusion in education, as well as recognising the significant progress that has been made. We then considered two of the biggest barriers that affect, not just LGBT+ people, but all people in schools: heteronormativity and cisnormativity. Considering how to challenge these barriers led us to the 'four pillars of inclusive education': language, curriculum, visibility, and representation. By developing each of these in our schools and classrooms, we disrupt cis/heteronormativity and create the windows and mirrors that give our students rich and empathetic understandings about the lives of LGBT+ people. In Chapters 6 and 7 we examined some of the challenges facing specific members of the LGBT+ community through the lens of intersectionality, and considered the importance of community and connection. We then reflected on the capacity we all have as leaders in a school and the power we have to affect change on a daily basis. The identity chapter provided us with an opportunity to reflect upon the ways in which our personal and professional identities intersect, thinking about our experiences of privilege. We then ended by thinking about the ways in which we can all commit to action to be better allies and advocates for the LGBT+ community.

In the Introduction, we explained that this book would be a combination of our experiences as educators and LGBT+ people, of the lived experiences of the people we have spoken to on our podcast, and of theory and research. The truth is, writing this book would not have been possible were it not for the inspirational people who have chosen generously to share their stories with us over the last three years. We want to thank every person who has been a part of this project – this book is as much yours as it is ours. Each person who has been on our podcast, and appeared in this book, is helping to reimagine our educational spaces as more LGBT+ inclusive. Together, they are the change. As Peter said in our final chapter, 'it is a collective effort. It is you, me, and all of us. It is we together. That is how change happens.'

As we thank our Pride & Progress community, we must also recognise that you are now part of this community, and we hope to meet you soon at one of our virtual or in person events! Please connect with us and follow our socials for upcoming events including the Pride & Progress Book Club, the LGBT+ Teacher Network, and to find out more about the training and support we can offer to schools.

Although this brings us to the end of the book, this is really just the beginning! The spheres of influence we have as teachers and educators are enormous. We have the ability to affect more change in one day than many people do in a year. By working together to reimagine our classrooms as more inclusive, we can have an immeasurable impact on the young people that we work with and the communities that we serve.

While this book focuses on how we make LGBT+ inclusive educational spaces, it is important to remember our broader goal as educators should remain to create spaces which are inclusive for *all* people. Our approaches to diversity, equity and inclusion should be holistic, and the argument this book has presented for greater LGBT+ equity and inclusion in schools, is an argument which benefits every person who occupies these spaces. In removing unhelpful social expectations, such as heteronormativity and cisnormativity, we can create a space where all people are free to be themselves. In making our language and curriculum inclusive, with real diverse visibility and representation, we create a space where all people can feel seen. In consciously exploring connection and community, we create spaces for every person to feel safe. In focusing on our leadership, allyship and advocacy, we can ensure every person feels supported. With all of those things in place, we are able to create inclusive educational spaces where every person in the school community feels free to be themselves, feels seen, feels safe, feels supported, and feels like they belong. In making this statement true for the LGBT+ people in your community, we help to make it true for all people.

In the Introduction to this book we shared with you the statement we used to launch the Pride & Progress podcast, and we want to conclude by sharing the same statement. It is as true now as it was at the beginning of this project.

> *We are living in a unique and pivotal moment for inclusive education. Now, for the first time ever, educators are strongly encouraged and enabled to make education, and our educational spaces, inclusive of LGBT+ lives. This requires a complete reimagining of what education could, and should, look like: an education that reflects the diverse society, allowing all people to see themselves and to feel they belong.*
>
> *Join us as we amplify the voices of these LGBT+ educators and allies, share their stories of pride and progress, and celebrate the true power of diversity in education.*

Thank you for being part of this journey. For reading this book, for listening to these stories, for learning, and for unlearning. Now, we hand it over to you. It is time for action.

So, are you ready? Time to begin…

PRIDE & PROGRESS PODCAST EPISODE LIST

Below is a list of all of the Pride & Progress episodes from seasons one and two. At the time of publishing Pride & Progress season three was being recorded, so there will be more episodes now available wherever you get your podcasts. All descriptions below were accurate at the time of publishing.

SEASON 1, EPISODE 1 – DR ADAM BRETT & JO BRASSINGTON

The creators of Pride & Progress come together to discuss why they started the podcast during this pivotal moment of change for LGBT+ inclusive education.

SEASON 1, EPISODE 2 – GEORGE WHITE

George (he/him) is a teacher of Religious Education, inclusion leader, and LGBTQ+ inclusion consultant. He joins us to share his experience as a trans man now teaching in the same Catholic school he attended as a student.

SEASON 1, EPISODE 3 – ALLISON ZIONTS

Allison (she/her) is a secondary school teacher and PhD researcher exploring LGBTQ+ safe spaces. She joins us to discuss her research, and share her experience as a bisexual, Jewish woman.

SEASON 1, EPISODE 4 – DOMINIC ARNALL

Dominic (he/him) was the CEO of LGBT+ young people's charity 'Just Like Us'at the time we spoke. He joins us to discuss the great work that Just Like Us does to support LGBT+ young people and schools.

SEASON 1, EPISODE 5 – B GUERRIERO

B (they/them) is a primary school teacher and LGBT+ youth worker with charity The Proud Trust. They join us to share their experience as a non-binary immigrant navigating a career in education.

SEASON 1, EPISODE 6 – KARAN BHUMBLA

Karan (he/him) is a secondary school science teacher. He joins us to share his experience as a gay, Indian science teacher working to be a positive representation for all facets of his identity.

SEASON 1, EPISODE 7 – ANDREW MOFFAT

Andrew (he/him) is an Assistant Headteacher, and creator of the resource 'No Outsiders: Everyone Different, Everyone Welcome'. Andrew joins us to share the story of No Outsiders, and explore how we can bring the wider school community on board with DEI work in schools.

SEASON 1, EPISODE 8 – KYRSTIE STUBBS

Kyrstie (she/her) is an inspirational former headteacher, now Deputy CEO, and an LGBT+ ally. She joins us to share how her leadership approaches diversity, equity, and inclusion in a holistic, and meaningful way.

SEASON 1, EPISODE 9 – CLAIRE BIRKENSHAW

Claire (she/her) is a former headteacher, academic, and incredible thinker. She joins us to share her experience as a trans woman, and to conceptualise some of the experiences of LGBT+ people with theory and thinking.

SEASON 1, EPISODE 10 – IAN EAGLETON & JAMES MAYHEW

Ian (he/him) was a primary school teacher for 13 years, and is now an author, and creator of The Reading Realm. James (he/him) is an artist and children's book illustrator. They join us to share their experience working on the beautifully inclusive fairytale: *Nen and The Lonely Fisherman*.

SEASON 1, EPISODE 11 – EILIDH VIZARD

Eilidh (she/her) is a secondary school science teacher. She joins us to discuss inclusive language, and representation for LGBT+ people, and women in STEM.

SEASON 1, EPISODE 12 – ADAM BRESLIN

Adam (he/him) is a science teacher and PhD researcher exploring LGBT+ rights and activism in education. He joins us to discuss the power that every teacher, child, and young person has to change the world through gentle acts of activism.

SEASON 1, EPISODE 13 – TROY JENKINSON

Troy (he/him) is a primary school headteacher and children's book author. He joins us to share his experience as an early career teacher during Section 28, and now as an inclusive leader.

SEASON 1, EPISODE 14 – HANNAH WILSON

Hannah (she/her) is a former headteacher, coach, trainer, and co-founder of Diverse Educators. She joins us to share her experience as an LGBT+ ally supporting diversity, equity, and inclusion with Diverse Educators.

SEASON 1, EPISODE 15 – SCOTTY CARTWRIGHT

Scotty (he/him) is an early career English teacher, who was a trainee when we spoke. He joins us to discuss his experience as a gay man joining the teaching profession.

SEASON 1, EPISODE 16 – DR ADAM BRETT & JO BRASSINGTON

The creators of Pride & Progress are joined by special friend of the show George White to reflect on the first season of the show, and to discuss what is to come next.

SEASON 2, EPISODE 1 – PROFESSOR EMERITUS SUE SANDERS & LYNNE NICHOLLS

Sue (she/her) is an inspirational educator and the co-founder of LGBT+ History Month. Lynne (she/her) is the Chair of Trustees for charity Schools Out. They join us to discuss the history of LGBT+ inclusive education, LGBT+ History Month, and the work of Schools Out.

SEASON 2, EPISODE 2 – HELEN RICHARDSON

Helen Richardson (she/her) is a deputy headteacher and led the diversity network for her school's Trust. Helen joins us to share her experience growing up during Section 28, and now working as an out, lesbian educator.

SEASON 2, EPISODE 3 – DR SHAUN DELLENTY

Shaun (he/him) is a multi-award-winning educator, LGBT+ inclusion advocate, trainer, inspirational speaker, and author. He joins us to share his experience as a gay primary school teacher, now supporting LGBT+ inclusion through training and consultancy.

SEASON 2, EPISODE 4 – EDEL CRONIN & AARON BROOKS

Edel (she/her) is a vice principal and works alongside English teacher and Head of House Aaron (he/him). They join us to share their experience working together to run an LGBTQ+ club for students in their school.

SEASON 2, EPISODE 5 – BENNIE KARA

Bennie (she/her) is a deputy headteacher, author, and co-founder of Diverse Educators. Bennie joins us to discuss her book, her role in Diverse Educators, and to reflect on intersectionality and her experiences as a gay Asian woman.

SEASON 2, EPISODE 6 – PROFESSOR CATHERINE LEE

Catherine (she/her) was a PE teacher before stepping into academia at Anglia Ruskin University. She joins us to discuss her experience as a lesbian PE teacher during Section 28, her current research into LGBT+ leadership, and setting up the Courageous Leaders programme.

SEASON 2, EPISODE 7 – DANIEL TOMLINSON-GRAY

Daniel (he/him) is a secondary teacher and co-founder of LGBTed. He joins us to discuss the origins of LGBTed, and their book: *Big Gay Adventures in Education*.

SEASON 2, EPISODE 8 – *HEARTSTOPPER* SPECIAL

In this episode the hosts of Pride & Progress assemble some special friends of the show to discuss the Netflix series *Heartstopper*, and the impact this story is having in schools.

SEASON 2, EPISODE 9 – FISAYO AKINADE

Fisayo (he/him) is a brilliant actor of both screen and stage, and plays Mr Ajayi in the Netflix show *Heartstopper*. He joins us to discuss his career in acting, and his role in *Heartstopper* portraying an LGBT+ educator.

SEASON 2, EPISODE 10 – CHARLOTTE FEATHER

Charlotte (she/her) is an educator, researcher, and the founder of the LGBTQ+ Primary Hub. She joins us to discuss her experience growing up as a bisexual woman in a rural area, and her research into the experiences of LGBTQ+ early career teachers.

SEASON 2, EPISODE 11 – DAVID LOWBRIDGE-ELLIS

David (he/they) is a headteacher, writer and trainer. He joins us to share brilliant tips on how to make educational spaces more inclusive, and how to be an effective and authentic leader.

SEASON 2, EPISODE 12 – NICK KITCHENER-BENTLEY

Nick (he/him) is a secondary school lead practitioner and teacher of drama, inclusion and English. He joins us to discuss his experiences, and how connecting with other LGBT+ educators can be transformational.

SEASON 2, EPISODE 13 – PROFESSOR PAUL BAKER

Paul (he/him) is a Professor of English Language and a researcher and writer. Paul joins us to discuss his latest book: *Outrageous!*, which charts the story of Section 28 and the battle for LGBT+ education.

SEASON 2, EPISODE 14 – PETER TATCHELL

Peter (he/him) has dedicated his life to campaigning for human rights and has been involved in LGBT+ activism for over 50 years. He joins us to share his life experience fighting for equity.

SPECIAL EPISODE – NEU LGBT+ EDUCATORS CONFERENCE

In this episode the hosts of Pride & Progress capture the NEU's LGBT+ Educators Conference 2022, where the conference theme was 'Defending our Community'. During this episode you can hear from Just Like Us, Olly Pike, Schools Out UK, Stonewall, Trans Actual, Kacey De Gruit, Denise Henry, and Divina De Campo.

SPECIAL EPISODE – DIVINA DE CAMPO

Divina (he/she/they) is an actor, singer, performer, drag artist, and member of *Drag Race* royalty. They join us to discuss their experiences of education, both as a student and later as a teacher.

INDEX